SEASONED COOKING
of KENTUCKY

A collection of Kentucky Monthly Recipes

SEASONED COOKING
of KENTUCKY

A collection of Kentucky Monthly Recipes

Seasoned Cooking of Kentucky is published by
Kentucky Monthly.

PUBLISHER **Stephen M. Vest**
EXECUTIVE EDITOR **Kim Butterweck**
ASSOCIATE EDITOR **Patricia Ranft**
CONTRIBUTING EDITORS **Madelynn Coldiron, Ted
Sloan** and **Kay Vest**
PROJECT MANAGER **Kendall Shelton**

CREATIVE DIRECTOR **Kelli Schreiber**
DESIGN ASSISTANT **Rebecca Redding**
PHOTOGRAPHY **Wales Hunter**
FOOD PREPARATION & STYLING **Sullivan University
chefs and students**

DIRECTOR OF RETAIL SALES **Lindsey McKinney**

This project was produced in partnership with
McClanahan Publishing House, Inc., Kuttawa, Ky,
www.kybooks.com

ISBN 13: 978-1-934898-14-7
Library of Congress Card Catalog Number 2011919477

All book order correspondence should be addressed to:

Kentucky Monthly
P.O. Box 559
Frankfort, KY 40602-0559

1-888-329-0053
www.kentuckymonthly.com

Manufactured in the United States of America

SPRING

As soft green begins to blanket the Commonwealth and wildflowers dot the landscape with color, Kentuckians display their triumph over winter melancholy with celebrations for which we're known around the world. Our collection of spring recipes reflects the social and festive ambiance of the season.

An homage to our horse racing heritage, culinary creations, such as Winning Ticket Breakfast Casserole, Derby Afternoon Cheese Straws, Steeplechase Pasta Salad and Mint Julep Cheesecake, showcase the exuberance of the season. Bright and flavorful dishes, including Watercress Soup, Bluegrass Asparagus Salad, Spring Vegetable Risotto and Coconut Lemon Cake, highlight the very essence of spring.

Prepare, share and enjoy these epicurean celebrations of the rebirth of the earth and the excitement of springtime in Kentucky.

Cheese *and* Bacon Stuffed New Potatoes

MAKES 8-10 SERVINGS

20 small **new potatoes**
Salt and **pepper** to taste
2 cups **cheddar cheese**, shredded
3 ounces **bacon**, crumbled
1 cup **sour cream with chives**

1 Boil potatoes in skins until done, approximately 15 minutes.

2 Drain, cool and halve.

3 Scoop out some of the center of each potato with a small spoon.

4 Salt and pepper the shells and sprinkle with cheese.

5 Top shells with bacon crumbles.

6 Place on a baking sheet and bake at 350°F until cheese is melted, about 10-15 minutes.

7 Remove and allow to cool slightly, then top each with a dollop of sour cream.

Country Ham *and* Asparagus Tartlets

MAKES 18 TARTLETS

Tart Shells
3 ounces **cream cheese**
4 tablespoons **butter**
¾ cup **all-purpose flour**
¼ cup **cornmeal**

Filling
¾ cup **Swiss cheese**, grated
1 tablespoon **all-purpose flour**
1 **egg**
⅓ cup **cream**
½ cup cooked **country ham,** minced
18 fresh **asparagus** tips, 1 inch long

1 Mix together the cream cheese and butter. Blend in the flour and cornmeal. Cover and chill for 1 hour.

2 Remove dough from refrigerator and shape into 1-inch balls. Place in miniature muffin tins and shape with thumb into tart shells. Set aside.

Filling

1 Mix together the cheese and flour.

2 Whisk together the egg and cream; add cheese mixture and ham.

3 Spoon into shells and bake at 425°F for 7 minutes. Top each tartlet with an asparagus tip.

4 Return to oven and reduce temperature to 300°F. Cover and bake an additional 17 minutes.

Loaded Stuffed Mushrooms

8 ounces whole **white mushrooms** or **baby portabella mushrooms**

4 ounces **Neufchâtel** or **cream cheese**

2 tablespoons **chives**, fresh or dried

2 tablespoons **bacon** pieces

¼ cup **Colby-Jack cheese**, shredded

1 Preheat oven to 350°F.

2 Wash the mushrooms and remove stems; set aside to drain.

3 Combine remaining ingredients in a small bowl and, using a small spatula, stuff the mushroom caps.

4 Place the mushrooms in a lightly greased 9x9-inch glass baking dish.

5 Bake for 20-25 minutes or until cheese filling begins to brown.

Derby Afternoon Cheese Straws

MAKES 6 DOZEN STRAWS

½ pound **sharp cheddar cheese**, grated

¼ pound **butter**, softened

⅛ teaspoon **cayenne pepper**

1½ cups self-rising **flour**

Paprika

Salt

1 Combine the cheese, butter, cayenne pepper and flour in a bowl; mix into a soft, pliable dough. Add a few drops of water if needed.

2 Roll the dough on a lightly floured board; cut the dough into ½-inch strips using a sharp knife or pizza cutter.

3 Place the straws on an uncoated baking sheet; bake at 325°F for about 20 minutes.

4 Allow to cool and sprinkle lightly with the paprika and salt. Store straws in an airtight container between sheets of waxed paper.

Ham *and* Cheese Buttermilk Biscuits

MAKES 10 BISCUITS

¼ cup **butter**
2 cups **self-rising flour**
¼ cup **buttermilk**
8 ounces **sour cream**
1 cup **Swiss cheese,** shredded
1 cup cooked **country ham**, finely chopped

1 Cut butter into flour with pastry blender until mixture is crumbly.

2 Add buttermilk, sour cream, cheese and ham, stirring until dry ingredients are moistened.

3 Turn dough out onto a lightly floured surface; knead three to four times.

4 Roll dough to ¾-inch thickness; cut with a 2½-inch round cutter and place on a ungreased baking sheet.

5 Bake biscuits at 425°F for 12 to 14 minutes.

6 Brush with melted butter if desired.

White Bean *and* Thyme Focaccia Wedges

3 medium **onions**, thinly sliced

¼ teaspoon **black pepper**, coarsely ground

1 tablespoon **olive oil**

¾ cup canned **white beans**, rinsed and drained

½ cup **dry white wine**

1 teaspoon **dried thyme**, crushed

4 6-inch **Italian bread shells** such as Boboli

Red sweet pepper julienned, *optional*

Fresh marjoram, *optional*

1 In a large skillet, cook the onions and black pepper in the oil over a medium-high heat, uncovered, for 7 minutes or until the onions turn brown. Remove the onions from the skillet and set aside.

2 Add the beans to the skillet; cook for 1 minute.

3 Add the wine and thyme; reduce heat and simmer, uncovered, for 3 to 4 minutes or until liquid is reduced by half.

4 Mash the bean mixture slightly.

5 Spread the bean mixture over the bread shells; top with the onions.

6 Bake at 450°F for 10 minutes. Cut into wedges. Garnish with red pepper and marjoram, if desired.

Shrimp *and* Lobster Bisque

MAKES 5-6 SERVINGS

2 steamed fresh **lobster tails**

4 tablespoons **butter**

1 small white **onion**, finely chopped

2 stalks **celery**, finely chopped

2 cloves **garlic**, minced

⅓ cup all-purpose **flour**

3 cups **chicken broth**

½ pound medium-size fresh **shrimp**, steamed, peeled, deveined, and chopped

2 cups **half & half**

10-ounce can **tomato soup**

1 teaspoon **cayenne pepper**

½ teaspoon **salt**

½ teaspoon ground **white pepper**

⅛ teaspoon fresh **nutmeg**

1 Remove lobster meat from shell; coarsely chop and set aside.

2 In a large saucepan, melt butter over medium heat. Add onion, celery and garlic. Cook for 5 minutes, stirring occasionally.

3 Stir in flour; cook for 2 minutes.

4 Stir in chicken broth and cook for 10 minutes, stirring occasionally until thickened.

5 Add shrimp and lobster meat. Stir in half & half, tomato soup and seasonings. Cook for 10 minutes or until heated through, stirring occasionally.

6 Serve immediately.

Watercress Soup

MAKES 4 SERVINGS

2 bunches **watercress**
¾ pound **potatoes**
1 **onion**
2 pints **chicken stock**
1½ ounces **butter**
1 **bay leaf**
1 clove **garlic**, peeled
   optional
Salt and **pepper** to taste
3 tablespoons **crème fraiche**
Nutmeg, grated
Croutons

1 Wash watercress thoroughly in cold water and discard any tough stalks or yellow leaves.

2 Peel and coarsely chop potatoes and onion.

3 Place potatoes, onion, watercress, stock, butter, bay leaf and garlic into a large saucepan. Season with salt and pepper and bring the soup to a boil.

4 Cover and simmer until potatoes are soft.

5 Remove bay leaf; in small batches, transfer the soup to a blender or food processor and puree until smooth. Return the soup to the pan and warm through.

6 Serve in individual bowls and swirl in the crème fraiche. Sprinkle with a little freshly grated nutmeg and serve with rustic croutons.

Leaf Lettuce *with* Poppy Seed Dressing

MAKES 4 SERVINGS

1 head **red leaf lettuce**
1 head **green leaf lettuce**
1 cup **strawberries**, sliced
1 cup canned **mandarin oranges**, drained

Poppy Seed Dressing
1 teaspoon **dry mustard**
1 teaspoon **salt**
1 tablespoon **poppy seeds**
¾ cup **sugar**
½ cup **apple cider vinegar**
1 cup **salad oil**

1 Wash, drain and tear the red and green leaf lettuce into bite-size pieces.

2 Add strawberries and mandarin oranges to the leaf lettuce in either a large salad bowl or four individual servings and allow to chill.

Poppy Seed Dressing

1 Mix dry dressing ingredients, add the vinegar and then add the oil. Mix well and chill.

2 When ready to serve, top salads with the prepared poppy seed dressing.

This recipe comes to us from Rosalie Swann, proprietor of Lexington's Swann's Nest at Cygnet Farm.

Bluegrass Asparagus Salad

MAKES 10-12 SERVINGS

1 head **Bibb lettuce**, washed, drained and dried

2 pounds **asparagus**, trimmed & washed

2 **lemons**, juiced

¼ teaspoon **nutmeg**

1 medium **red onion**, chopped

6-ounce jar **sliced pimientos**, drained

3-ounce jar sliced pitted **black olives**, drained

8 ounces **blue cheese**, crumbled

¼ cup **extra virgin olive oil**

4-ounce jar **capers**, drained

Cracked black **pepper** to taste

1 Wash lettuce and arrange on a serving platter or in a salad bowl.

2 Bring a pot of water to a boil. Add half of the lemon juice. Add asparagus and blanch for four minutes or until spears are bright green.

3 Plunge asparagus in ice water to stop the cooking process. Drain, add more lemon juice and toss spears.

4 Sprinkle with nutmeg and toss again.

5 Arrange asparagus on lettuce. Top with red onions, pimientos, olives and blue cheese.

6 Mix olive oil and drained capers.

7 Pour mixture on top of the salad and add pepper to taste.

Submitted by Joan Sewell of Evansville, Ind., this recipe was the first-place overall winner in Kentucky Monthly's 2010 Recipe Contest.

Sunshine Citrus Spinach Salad

MAKES 4 SERVINGS

4 cups **spinach leaves**

16-ounce can **mandarin oranges**, drained

16-ounce can **grapefruit** segments, drained

½ **green pepper**, thinly sliced

4 ounces **walnuts**, chopped

1 cup **ranch dressing**

½ cup Kentucky **honey**

1 Wash spinach and dry.

2 Tear spinach into bite-size pieces and place on 4 salad plates. Top with fruit, pepper slivers and nuts.

3 Mix ranch dressing and honey in a small bowl.

4 Drizzle dressing mixture over fruit and spinach.

Mediterranean Layered Rice Salad

MAKES 8 SERVINGS

1 cup **whole-grain brown rice**, cooked

2 tablespoons **olive oil**

2 cups fresh **mushrooms**, sliced

¼ cup fresh **chives**

2 cups **broccoli florets**, blanched and drained

2 **red bell peppers**, chopped

2 **green onions**, chopped

12-ounce package **frozen green peas**, thawed

2 large **tomatoes**, peeled and sliced

1 cup **Havarti cheese**, shredded

Dressing

1½ cups **balsamic vinegar dressing**

¼ cup **orange marmalade**, or your favorite jelly or jam

1 Sauté the mushrooms and chives together in the olive oil.

2 Combine the dressing and the marmalade and stir well.

3 Mix ½ cup of the balsamic vinegar dressing mixture with the rice and mushroom mixture. Place ½ of this in the bottom of a large glass serving bowl.

4 Layer the broccoli, red peppers and green onions. Drizzle ½ cup of the dressing over the vegetables.

5 Top with remaining rice mixture. Layer the peas and tomatoes and drizzle with the remaining dressing.

6 Top with cheese, cover and refrigerate several hours before serving.

Early Garden Spinach Salad

MAKES 2 SERVINGS

6 cups fresh, young and tender **spinach** leaves

4 to 8 spears fresh **asparagus**

8 to 10 **green onions**, including the blades

8 to 10 fresh **chive** blades

4 hardboiled **eggs**

½ cup **bacon bits** or **bacon-flavored soy bits**

½ cup crushed **corn chips**, *optional*

Mustard Vinaigrette

1 medium **onion**

¾ cup **sugar**

1 teaspoon **salt**

1 teaspoon **dry mustard**

⅓ cup **white vinegar**

1 cup **canola oil**

1 Wash the vegetables, chop into bite-size pieces and toss in a salad bowl.

2 Chop shelled boiled eggs and add to garden vegetables.

Mustard Vinaigrette

1 Process all ingredients except oil together in a food processor. Turn on processor again and slowly pour canola oil through the chute. The mixture will emulsify and thicken.

2 Top with bacon bits and lightly toss salad with dressing.

Submitted by Jean Merrell of Madisonville, this recipe was the winner in the Starters category in Kentucky Monthly's 2010 Recipe Contest.

Clare Ann's Pasta Salad

MAKES 12 SERVINGS

12-ounce box **tri-colored spiral pasta**

9-ounce package frozen, **cheese-filled tortellini pasta**

2 small **zucchini**, diced

1 small **yellow squash**, diced

1 pound fresh **asparagus**

2 cups **broccoli florets**

8.5-ounce can **artichoke hearts**, quartered

3.8-ounce can **ripe black olives**, sliced

1 pint **cherry tomatoes**, cut in half

½ cup **fresh parsley**, chopped

16-ounce bottle **Italian dressing**

Feta cheese for garnish

1 Boil pastas according to package directions. Drain and cool.

2 Pour pastas into a large mixing bowl and add remaining ingredients, except the feta cheese.

3 Mix well, cover and refrigerate. Pasta will absorb the dressing.

4 Top with feta cheese just before serving.

This recipe comes to us from Tina Emrick of Sage Garden Café in Frankfort.

Steeplechase Pasta Salad

MAKES 4-6 SERVINGS

1 teaspoon **salt**

1 pound **fusilli** or **penne pasta**

1 tablespoon plus ⅓ cup **extra-virgin olive oil**

2 pounds ripe **tomatoes**, peeled, seeded and coarsely chopped

5 cloves **garlic**, minced

½ cup **basil**, coarsely chopped

¼ cup **Italian parsley**, finely chopped

3 tablespoons **red wine vinegar**

1 pound fresh **mozzarella cheese**, cut into 1-inch cubes

½ cup **Parmesan cheese**, grated

Salt and **pepper** to taste

1 Bring a large pot two-thirds full of water to a boil over high heat.

2 Add salt, and then add the pasta, stir well and cook until al dente (tender but firm to the bite)—about 7 to 10 minutes.

3 Drain the pasta, place in a serving bowl and stir in 1 tablespoon olive oil.

4 Combine tomatoes, garlic, basil, parsley, vinegar, ⅓ cup olive oil, mozzarella and Parmesan cheese in a large mixing bowl.

5 Add salt and pepper to taste and stir in pasta and mix well.

6 Cover and refrigerate until ready to enjoy.

From Sterling Bits: Bluegrass Equestrian Experience, *published by McClanahan Publishing House, for which Kathy Mayfield provided the culinary sections and Suzy F. Smith created equestrian drawings.*

Mixed Herbed Greens *with* Honey Mustard Dressing

MAKES 4-6 SERVINGS

8 ounces herbed **spring greens mix**
1 **carrot**, shredded
1 pint **cherry tomatoes**
1 cup **water chestnuts**, drained and rinsed

Honey Mustard Dressing
¾ cup **mayonnaise**
¼ cup **honey**
1 teaspoon **Worcestershire sauce**
3 tablespoons **spicy brown mustard**
1 teaspoon **lemon juice**

1 Arrange the greens on individual salad plates.

2 Top the greens with the carrots, tomatoes and water chestnuts.

3 Spoon dressing over each salad.

Honey Mustard Dressing
1 Whisk the mayonnaise, honey, Worcestershire sauce, mustard and lemon juice into a bowl.

2 Pour into a container with a tight-fitting lid and store in the refrigerator.

3 Shake well before using.

Makes 1 cup

Winning Ticket
Breakfast Casserole

MAKES 8-10 SERVINGS

1 pound **mild pork sausage**

½ cup **onion**, chopped

4 cups shredded **hash brown potatoes**

6 **eggs**, lightly beaten

2 cups **mild cheddar cheese**, shredded

1½ cups small-curd **cottage cheese**

1¼ cups **Swiss cheese**, shredded

Salt and **pepper** to taste

1 Brown the sausage and onion in a large skillet; drain.

2 Place the hash brown potatoes in the bottom of a coated 9x13-inch baking dish. Layer the sausage and onion mixture over the hash browns.

3 Combine the eggs and cheeses in a large bowl. Pour over the potatoes and sausage.

4 Sprinkle with salt and pepper. Bake, uncovered, at 350°F for 35 to 40 minutes or until the eggs are set and bubbly.

5 Let stand for 10 minutes before serving.

Sausage Cheese Grits

MAKES 8 SERVINGS

1 pound Grandma Broadbent's pork **sausage**

1 cup **quick-cooking grits**

1 small **onion**, chopped

⅓ cup **green pepper**, chopped

1½ cups **sharp cheddar cheese**, shredded

1 Cook grits according to package directions; set aside.

2 Crumble sausage in a large skillet; add onions and green pepper. Cook over medium heat until meat is brown and vegetables are tender. Drain well.

3 Combine grits, meat mixture and 1 cup of cheese.

4 Spoon into greased 10x6x2-inch baking dish. Bake at 350°F for 15 minutes.

5 Sprinkle with remaining cheese; bake for 5 minutes or until cheese melts.

Peppered Bacon-Wrapped Pork Tenderloin

MAKES 8 SERVINGS

¼ cup **butter**

¾ pound **mushrooms**, sliced

1 small **onion**, chopped

¼ cup **pecans**, chopped and toasted

2 12-ounce **pork tenderloins**, trimmed

1 teaspoon **salt**

1 teaspoon **ground black pepper**

8 slices Broadbent's peppered **bacon**

¼ cup firmly packed **brown sugar**

1 Melt butter in a large skillet over medium heat; add mushrooms and onions, and sauté 8 minutes or until tender. Stir in pecans and set aside.

2 Place pork between two sheets of plastic wrap; flatten to ¼-inch thick and remove plastic. Sprinkle with salt and pepper.

3 Spread the mushroom mixture evenly on one side of the tenderloin, leaving a ¼-inch border. Roll up and wrap 4 bacon slices around tenderloin and secure with wooden picks.

4 Place, seam side down, on greased rack in a roasting pan. Rub evenly with brown sugar.

5 Bake uncovered at 450°F for 15 minutes. Reduce temperature to 400°F and bake for an additional 15 minutes or until meat thermometer registers 160°F.

Curried Chicken, Spinach *and* Mushroom Casserole

MAKES 4 SERVINGS

5-ounce package fresh **baby spinach**

3 boneless, skinless **chicken breasts**

Salt and **pepper** to taste

Onion powder to taste

Garlic powder to taste

8 large **mushrooms**, chopped

7 **cherry tomatoes**, halved

4 tablespoons **butter**

1 cup grated **Parmesan cheese**

1 cup **heavy cream**

¼ teaspoon **curry powder**

Brown rice

1 Place the spinach in a coated 9x13-inch baking dish.

2 Slice the chicken in 2-inch strips and sprinkle with the salt, pepper, onion powder and garlic powder. Place the chicken on the top of the spinach.

3 Layer the mushrooms and tomatoes on the top of the chicken.

4 Melt the butter in a large skillet and add the cheese. Cook over medium heat until the cheese melts. Add the cream and cook about 5 minutes, stirring until well blended. Add the curry, stir and pour the mixture over the chicken.

5 Bake at 350°F for 45 to 60 minutes.

6 Serve over brown rice.

Grilled Turkey *with* Black Bean Salsa

MAKES 4 SERVINGS

1 teaspoon **chili powder**

1 teaspoon **cumin**

1 teaspoon **salt**

¼ teaspoon **cayenne pepper**

1 pound **turkey tenderloins**

Black Bean Salsa

⅓ cup **onion**, chopped

1 **jalapeño pepper**, seeded and minced

1 teaspoon **olive oil**

15-ounce can **black beans**, drained and rinsed

8.75-ounce can **corn**, drained

⅓ cup **tomato**, chopped

2 tablespoons fresh **cilantro**, chopped

1 **lime**

1 Combine the chili powder, cumin, salt and cayenne pepper in a small bowl.

2 Sprinkle half the mixture over the turkey.

3 Grill the tenderloins for 15 to 20 minutes, turning once, or until the meat is no longer pink in the center and a meat thermometer reads 160°F.

4 Allow tenderloins to stand 10 minutes.

5 Before serving, top with black bean salsa and a squeeze of lime juice.

Black Bean Salsa

1 Sauté the onion and jalapeño pepper in oil in a medium, nonstick skillet over a medium-high heat, 2 to 3 minutes or until onion softens.

2 Add the beans, corn, tomato, cilantro and remaining chili powder, cumin, salt and cayenne pepper mixture.

3 Cook 25 to 30 minutes or until the mixture is heated through.

Shrimp Cakes *with* Fresh Tartar Sauce

MAKES 4 SERVINGS

¾ pound fresh Gulf **shrimp**
4 **green onions**, sliced
2 tablespoons **extra virgin olive oil**
2 **eggs**, beaten
½ cup **panko bread crumbs**
3 ounces **French fried rings**, crushed finely
Salt and **pepper** to taste

Tartar Sauce
½ cup **mayonnaise**
½ small **onion**, chopped
2 tablespoons chopped **green pepper**
1 large **dill pickle**, chopped
2 tablespoons **green olives**, sliced

1 Place shrimp in boiling water and cook until they just turn pink. Remove from water, cool, peel and devein.

2 Cut shrimp into small pieces and set aside.

3 Pour 1 tablespoon oil into skillet and cook sliced green onions for about 2 minutes on medium high. Set aside.

4 Place ½ of the cut-up shrimp, eggs and onions into a food processor and mix. Pour mixture into a bowl; add the remaining shrimp and mix with panko crumbs.

5 Shape mixture into 4 patties and bread with onion rings.

6 Place patties over medium heat in a large skillet with 1 tablespoon oil. Cook until patty holds together well enough to be turned and cooked on the other side.

7 Remove patties when golden brown and drain on paper towels.

Tartar Sauce

1 Place all ingredients into a food processor and combine until well mixed.

2 Cover and refrigerate.

Makes about 1 cup.

Country Ham Salad

MAKES 5 CUPS

4 cups **country ham**, cooked

1 large **Granny Smith apple**, peeled and finely chopped

1 cup **celery**, finely chopped

1 bunch **green onions**, sliced, using about 2 inches of green tops

1½ teaspoons **black pepper**, coarsely ground

1¼ cups real **mayonnaise**

3 tablespoons **Dijon mustard**

1 Grind the country ham in a food processor and place in a large mixing bowl.

2 Add the chopped apple, celery and green onions.

3 Stir in the black pepper, mayonnaise and Dijon mustard.

4 Mix thoroughly and chill for at least 1 hour.

5 To serve, spread on small, baked party rolls or serve as a spread with crackers.

Chicken *and* Mushroom Paprika

MAKES 4 SERVINGS

2 tablespoons **olive oil**

3 boneless, skinless **chicken breast** halves, sliced in 1-inch squares

½ **onion**, chopped

2 cups **mushrooms**, sliced

1 clove **garlic**, minced

½ teaspoon **salt**

¼ teaspoon **pepper**

¾ to 1 cup **chicken broth**

8 ounces **sour cream**

2 teaspoons ground **paprika**

Wild rice

1 Pour oil in a skillet and sauté chicken, stirring constantly for 5 minutes or until no longer pink. Set chicken aside, cover, and keep warm.

2 Add a little more oil to the pan and gently sauté the onion, sliced mushrooms and garlic for about 3 minutes.

3 Add salt, pepper and broth, and return the chicken to the skillet.

4 Cook over medium heat about 2 minutes; add sour cream and paprika and simmer (do not boil) until heated through.

5 Serve over wild rice.

Horseradish Crusted Salmon

MAKES 4 SERVINGS

1 cup **Italian dressing**

1 cup **honey**

4 **salmon fillets**

2 tablespoons **horseradish**

1 cup fresh **parsley**, chopped

1 tablespoon **lemon zest**

2 tablespoons **whole grain mustard**

2 tablespoons fresh **garlic**, chopped

2 tablespoons **olive oil**

Salt and **pepper** to taste

1 cup **panko bread crumbs**

1 Mix dressing and honey together in a shallow bowl. Place salmon in the mixture, refrigerate, and marinate for 6 hours, but no longer than that.

2 Remove salmon from marinade, shake off excess liquid and place fillets in a hot skillet with a small amount of oil. Cook until the fish becomes a nice caramel color. Remove from the heat and set aside.

3 Mix together the horseradish, parsley, lemon zest, mustard, garlic, oil, salt, pepper and bread crumbs. The mixture should be able to hold its shape but not be wet (adjust with more bread crumbs if too wet or with mustard if too dry).

4 Place salmon onto a baking sheet and place ¼ of bread crumb mixture on top of each fillet, lightly pressing mixture to stay in place.

5 Bake at 375°F until topping is just brown.

Rosemary Roasted Vegetables

MAKES 12 SERVINGS

1 pound **Brussels sprouts**

12 ounces **green beans**

6 **green onions**, trimmed and diced

12 fresh **rosemary sprigs**

8 slices **bacon**, partially cooked, drained and cut into pieces

2 tablespoons **olive oil**

Salt and **black pepper** to taste

1 **lemon**, halved

1 Wash the green beans and Brussels sprouts; drain.

2 Cook the Brussels sprouts in a small amount of lightly salted boiling water for 3 minutes.

3 Add the green beans; cook for 5 additional minutes and drain.

4 Place the vegetables in a shallow roasting pan. Add the green onions and rosemary sprigs; toss to combine.

5 Top with the bacon. Drizzle the vegetable mixture with the olive oil. Sprinkle with salt and pepper.

6 Roast, uncovered, at 425°F for 20 minutes or until the vegetables are crisp-tender and bacon is crisp.

7 Transfer the vegetables to a serving platter. Squeeze lemon juice over them.

Spring Vegetable Risotto

MAKES 4 SERVINGS

7 cups **water**

3 teaspoons **salt**, plus 2 teaspoons for water

Black pepper, freshly ground

½ cup **butter**

8 ounces fresh **mushrooms**, sliced

1 **shallot**, diced

1½ cups **Arborio rice**

½ cup **dry vermouth**

3 to 4 sprigs fresh **thyme**

4 ounces **asparagus**, cut into ¼-inch pieces, with woody part removed

½ cup **Parmesan cheese**, grated

1 cup **peas**

2 tablespoons **lemon juice**

1 Bring the water to a simmer and add the 2 teaspoons of salt. Keep on a low simmer.

2 Heat 2 tablespoons of the butter in a large skillet over medium-high heat and add the mushrooms. Cook, stirring occasionally, until crispy and browned. Season with salt and pepper to taste, and set aside.

3 In a large saucepan, add another 2 tablespoons of the butter over medium-high heat and let brown slightly until nutty.

4 Add the shallot and cook for 2 minutes or until translucent.

5 Add the rice and stir so that it is coated with the butter and glossy, about 1 minute.

6 Stir in the remaining salt. Add the vermouth and cook, stirring constantly with a wooden spoon, until the vermouth is absorbed by the rice.

7 Add the thyme sprigs. Ladle in ½ cup of the simmering water and stir constantly, until the rice again absorbs the liquid, adjusting the heat to maintain a gentle simmer.

8 Continue ladling in ½ cup of water at a time, stirring between additions and letting the rice absorb the liquid before adding more.

9 Add the asparagus.

10 When rice is tender, but al dente, after about 20 minutes of cooking time, stop adding water. Vigorously beat in the remaining butter and cheese.

11 Add the mushrooms, peas and lemon juice and stir just until heated through.

12 Remove from the heat. Let it rest for a minute or so before serving.

Brown Rice *with* Shredded Carrots

MAKES 4 SERVINGS

2 cups instant **brown rice**

2 cups **water**

1 cup **carrots**, shredded

2 teaspoons **beef bouillon**

1 Combine the rice, water, beef bouillon and carrots and cook in a covered saucepan on high until the mixture boils.

2 Turn down heat to low and continue to cook, covered, for about 15 minutes until all the liquid is absorbed.

Pesto Potatoes

MAKES 4 SERVINGS

9 **red potatoes**, scrubbed but not peeled
¼ cup **basil pesto**
Salt and **pepper** to taste

1 Slice potatoes in quarters.

2 Place in a large mixing bowl; stir in the pesto until all the potatoes are coated.

3 Sprinkle with salt and pepper.

4 Pour into a baking dish. Bake in a 350°F oven for one hour, turning every 15 minutes.

Quick Lemon Bars

MAKES 9 TWO-INCH SQUARES

16.5-ounce package **Betty Crocker Sunkist Lemon Bar Mix**
Lemon juice
Powdered sugar
Fresh mint

1 Line an 8x8-inch square pan with foil.

2 Prepare lemon bars according to package instructions, substituting the lemon juice for the water.

3 Cool and chill.

4 Cut into 2-inch squares. Dust with powdered sugar just before serving. Garnish with sprigs of fresh mint.

Apricot Oatmeal Cookies

MAKES 48 COOKIES

2 sticks **butter**, softened
1 cup **light brown sugar**
¾ cup **sugar**
2 **eggs**
1½ cups all-purpose **flour**
1½ teaspoons **kosher salt**
1 teaspoon **baking powder**
¼ teaspoon freshly ground **nutmeg**
3 cups **old-fashioned oats**
1½ cups **dried apricots**, cut in small pieces (**cranberries** or **raisins** work well, too)

1 Beat the butter with an electric mixer until creamy.

2 Add sugars to the butter and beat until fluffy, about 3 minutes.

3 Beat in eggs, one at a time.

4 Sift together the flour, salt, baking powder and nutmeg.

5 Add the flour mixture to the butter mixture and stir with a wooden spoon or spatula to blend.

6 Stir in oats and dried fruit.

7 Form dough into 1-inch balls and place on a baking sheet covered with parchment or foil.

8 Bake at 350°F for approximately 12 minutes, until the bottom edges turn brown. The cookies will still be soft and feel a bit undercooked.

9 If using baking paper, slide off onto a cooling rack. Otherwise, allow cookies to cool for 2 minutes on the baking sheet and then remove to the rack.

10 When cooled, store in an airtight container.

Bourbon Cheesecake Brownies

MAKES 12 TWO-INCH SQUARES

1½ pounds **semisweet chocolate**

6 ounces **butter**

1½ cups **sugar**

12 **eggs**

6 cups **flour**

1 tablespoon **vanilla**

⅓ cup Kentucky **bourbon**

24-ounces **cream cheese**

1½ cups **sugar**

2 tablespoons **flour**

1 tablespoon **vanilla**

½ cup **sour cream**

1 Melt the chocolate in a heavy saucepan over medium heat, stirring constantly.

2 Cream butter and sugar together in a large mixing bowl. Add the first six eggs, one at a time, and beat well.

3 Combine the flour with the egg mixture. Add the vanilla and bourbon, and mix. Pour in the melted chocolate and stir until smooth. Pour into a prepared 9x13-inch pan.

4 Beat cream cheese in a large mixing bowl at high speed until light and fluffy. Gradually add the sugar, beating well.

5 Add the remaining six eggs, one at a time until well incorporated. Stir in the flour and vanilla. Fold in the sour cream.

6 Gently pour the cream cheese mixture on top of the chocolate mixture in the pan, being careful not to disturb it.

7 Bake in a preheated oven at 375°F for 45-50 minutes, until set.

Mint Julep Cheesecake

MAKES 10 SERVINGS

2 cups **chocolate graham crackers**, crushed

4 tablespoons **butter**, melted

2 8-ounce packages **cream cheese**

1½ cups **sour cream**

½ cup **sugar**

2 **eggs**

2 teaspoons Kentucky **bourbon**

2 tablespoons **butter**, melted

3 ounces **cream cheese**

4 tablespoons **butter**

2 cups **powdered sugar**

3 teaspoons **mint extract**

2 drops **green food coloring**

1 cup **semi-sweet chocolate morsels**

¾ cup **heavy cream**

Fresh mint for garnish

1 Mix together crushed graham crackers with melted butter; line the bottom and ¼ to ½ up the sides of a 9-inch springform pan with the crumbs.

2 Bake at 350°F for 10 minutes. Remove and cool.

3 Combine 2 eight-ounce packages of cream cheese and sugar in the food processor and mix until smooth.

4 Add the sour cream, eggs and bourbon and mix well. Add the butter and mix again.

5 Pour ingredients into the cooled crust. Bake at 350°F for 1 hour. Cool and refrigerate.

6 Combine the additional 3 ounces of cream cheese, butter and powdered sugar in a food processor and mix well. Add the mint flavoring and food coloring and mix. Spread this layer onto the baked and cooled cheesecake. Refrigerate.

7 Melt the chocolate morsels in a double boiler and add cream, stirring until melted and mixed. Refrigerate, stirring every few minutes until the mixture is thickened like cream cheese.

8 Spread over the green layer of the cheesecake and refrigerate until set.

Chocolate Coffee Cups

MAKES 4 SERVINGS

1 cup **skim milk**

½ cup **whipping cream**

5 tablespoons **Splenda**

2 **eggs**, beaten

2 teaspoons **instant coffee granules**

2 teaspoons **cocoa**

1 teaspoon **vanilla extract**

Whipped topping for garnish

Cinnamon sugar for garnish

1 Whisk the milk, cream, sweetener, eggs, coffee and cocoa. Add vanilla extract and stir well.

2 Pour into 4 small ramekins placed in a 9x13-inch baking dish. Pour water into the baking dish so that it comes halfway up the ramekins. Bake at 350°F for 25 to 45 minutes, until tops are crusty brown.

3 Carefully remove from hot water, cool and place in the refrigerator for at least 2 hours to chill.

4 Top with whipped topping and a sprinkle of cinnamon sugar.

Chocolate Chip Cake

MAKES 4 SERVINGS

18.75-ounce **yellow cake mix**

3-ounce package **instant vanilla pudding**

3-ounce package **instant chocolate pudding**

4 **eggs**

1½ cups **water**

½ cup **oil**

6-ounce package **chocolate chips**

Frosting, powdered sugar or **strawberries**, *optional*

1 Combine the cake mix and puddings in a large bowl; stir until mixed.

2 Add the eggs, water and oil; blend well. Beat for 2 minutes at medium speed.

3 Add the chocolate chips and stir, using a spoon.

4 Pour mixture into a coated and floured Bundt pan. Bake at 325°F for 1 hour. Cool before removing from pan.

5 Ice with your favorite frosting or sprinkle with powdered sugar and garnish with strawberries.

Walnut Bourbon Balls

MAKES 3½ DOZEN

1 cup **powdered sugar**

2½ cups **vanilla wafers**, finely crushed

2 tablespoons **cocoa**

1 cup **walnuts**, finely chopped

3 tablespoons **white corn syrup**

¼ cup Kentucky **bourbon**

1 Mix together the powdered sugar, vanilla wafers, cocoa and walnuts in a large mixing bowl.

2 Add the syrup and bourbon.

3 Pinch off mixture and roll into 1-inch balls.

4 Roll balls in powdered sugar and store in an airtight container.

Kathy Cary's Coconut Lemon Cake

MAKES 1 THREE-LAYER CAKE

1 cup **unsalted butter**, softened

2 cups **sugar**

4 large **eggs**, separated

3 cups all-purpose **flour**

1 tablespoon **baking powder**

1 cup **milk**

1 teaspoon **vanilla extract**

⅛ teaspoon **salt**

Coconut

1 Beat butter at medium speed with an electric mixer until fluffy; gradually add sugar.

2 Add egg yolks, one at a time, beating after each addition.

3 Combine flour and baking powder; add to butter mixture alternately with milk, beginning and ending with flour mixture.

4 Beat at low speed until blended after each addition.

5 Stir in vanilla; set batter aside.

6 Beat egg whites and salt at high speed with mixer until stiff peaks form.

7 Stir about one-third of the egg whites into the batter, and then fold in the remaining egg whites.

8 Spoon batter into three greased and floured 9-inch round pans.

9 Bake at 350°F for 18 to 20 minutes or until a wooden pick inserted into center comes out clean.

10 Cool in pans on wire racks 10 minutes; remove from pans and cool completely.

11 Spread lemon filling between layers.

12 Spread fluffy white frosting on top and sides of cake.

13 Sprinkle top and sides with coconut.

Kathy Cary is chef and owner of Lilly's, A Kentucky Bistro, in Louisville.

Lemon Filling

1 cup **sugar**
¼ cup **cornstarch**
1 cup boiling **water**
4 **egg yolks**, lightly beaten
⅓ cup fresh **lemon juice**
2 tablespoons **butter**

Fluffy White Frosting

1 cup **sugar**
1½ cups **water**
2 tablespoons **light corn syrup**
4 **egg whites**
¼ teaspoon **cream of tartar**

Lemon Filling

1 Combine sugar and cornstarch in a medium saucepan; stir in water.

2 Cook over medium heat, stirring constantly, until sugar and cornstarch dissolve, about 3 minutes.

3 Gradually stir about one-fourth of hot mixture into yolks; add to remaining hot mixture, stirring constantly with a wire whisk.

4 Stir in lemon juice.

5 Cook, stirring constantly, until mixture is thickened.

6 Remove from heat; stir in butter and let cool, stirring occasionally.

Yields 1⅔ cups.

Fluffy White Frosting

1 Combine sugar, water and syrup in a small, heavy saucepan; cook over medium heat, stirring constantly, until clear.

2 Cook, without stirring, until mixture reaches soft-ball stage or candy thermometer registers 240°F.

3 Beat egg whites and cream of tartar at high speed with an electric mixer until soft peaks form; slowly add syrup mixture, beating constantly.

4 Beat until stiff peaks form and frosting is desired consistency.

Yields 7 cups.

Panna Cotta

MAKES 6 SERVINGS

⅓ cup **skim milk**
¼-ounce envelope
unflavored gelatin
2½ cups **heavy cream**
½ cup **sugar**
1½ teaspoons **vanilla
extract**
Fresh berries, *optional*

1 Pour the milk into a small bowl and stir in the gelatin. Set aside.

2 Combine the heavy cream and sugar in a saucepan over medium heat. Bring to a full boil, watching carefully, as the cream will rise quickly to the top of the pan.

3 Pour the gelatin/milk mixture into the cream, stirring until completely dissolved. Cook for 1 minute, stirring constantly.

4 Remove from the heat and stir in the vanilla extract; pour into six individual ramekin dishes.

5 Cool the ramekins, uncovered, at room temperature. When cool, cover with plastic wrap and refrigerate at least 4 hours, but preferably overnight, before serving.

6 Garnish with fresh berries, if desired.

Lemon-Scented Strawberry Shortcake *with* Rhubarb Sauce

MAKES 8 SERVINGS

8 **biscuits**
Rhubarb sauce
**Lemon-scented
strawberries**
Whipped cream

Jerry's Sweet Biscuit Dough
2 cups all-purpose **flour**
1 teaspoon **baking
powder**
½ teaspoon **baking soda**
¼ teaspoon **salt**
¼ cup **sugar**
4 tablespoons **unsalted
butter**
1 cup **sour cream**
¼ cup **whole milk**

1 Cut each biscuit in half using a serrated knife.

2 Spoon a few tablespoons of rhubarb sauce on plate and place the bottom half of the biscuit onto sauce.

3 Spoon more sauce onto biscuit bottom followed by a few spoonfuls of lemon-scented strawberries.

4 Spoon a large dollop of whipped cream onto berries and cap with biscuit top.

5 Scatter a few berries around the plate for garnish.

Jerry's Sweet Biscuit Dough

1 Sift flour, baking powder, baking soda and salt into a medium mixing bowl.

2 Stir in sugar.

3 Cut in butter with a pastry fork until mixture resembles coarse meal.

4 Stir in sour cream and milk.

5 Gently mix until ingredients form a gooey mixture.

6 Scoop mixture into 8 evenly spaced mounds on a cookie sheet lined with parchment paper.

7 Sprinkle tops with sugar.

8 Bake at 425°F until lightly browned, about 15 minutes. Let cool.

Rhubarb Sauce

3 cups **fresh rhubarb**

4 cups **water**

1 cup **sugar**

¼ cup **honey**

1 tablespoon **balsamic vinegar**

1 cup **strawberries**, sliced

Lemon-Scented Strawberries

1 pint fresh **strawberries**

1 **lemon**

¼ cup **sugar**

Rhubarb Sauce

1 Wash rhubarb and chop into small chunks.

2 Combine with water in a saucepan and boil on high until rhubarb is very soft (add more water if needed).

3 Add sugar, honey, vinegar and strawberries.

4 Cook on medium heat until sugar and honey are dissolved.

5 Blend mixture on high in a processor until smooth. Cool before serving.

Lemon-Scented Strawberries

1 Remove green stems from strawberries and cut into quarters.

2 Place strawberries into a medium-size mixing bowl.

3 Using a zester or fine grater, add half the lemon's zest and the juice from half the lemon.

4 Add sugar and mix gently.

5 Let strawberries sit for 30 minutes or more before serving.

Chocolate Pecan No-Bake Cookies

MAKES 6 SERVINGS

2 cups **sugar**

¼ cup **cocoa**

¼ pound **unsalted butter**

½ cup **milk**

½ cup **peanut butter**

1½ cups **old-fashioned oatmeal**

½ tablespoon **vanilla**

1½ cups **pecans**, chopped

1 Mix together the sugar, cocoa, butter and milk in a large pot. Bring to a boil, stirring constantly; continue boiling for 1½ minutes.

2 Remove pot from the stove and stir in peanut butter until incorporated.

3 Stir in the oatmeal, vanilla and pecans. Mix until ingredients are combined.

4 Scoop out mixture a tablespoonful at a time onto parchment paper-lined pans and allow to fully cool.

5 Store in an airtight container.

Marsha Burton's Woodford Pudding

MAKES 12 SERVINGS

1 cup **butter**, melted and cooled

6 **eggs**

1 cup **buttermilk**

2 cups WindStone Farms **seedless blackberry jam**

2 cups **sugar**

2 cups all-purpose **flour**

2 teaspoons **baking soda**

2 teaspoons **cinnamon**

Bourbon Sauce

2 cups **brown sugar**

2 cups **cream**

2 sticks **butter**

¼ cup Woodford Reserve **bourbon**

1 Mix butter, eggs and buttermilk in a large bowl; stir in jam.

2 Combine dry ingredients and add to liquid; mix until creamy and pour into a large, greased Bundt pan.

3 Bake at 350°F for 45 minutes or until pudding is set.

Bourbon Sauce

1 Combine brown sugar and cream in a saucepan and bring to a boil, stirring constantly. Add butter and whisk until blended; add bourbon.

2 Pour sauce over warm pudding, setting aside some extra for drizzling when served.

This recipe comes to us from Marsha Burton, owner of Louisville's 1853 Inn at Woodhaven.

Midday Mocha Cooler

MAKES 1 SERVING

1 package **Starbucks Via**
½ cup low-fat **chocolate frozen yogurt**
1 cup **skim milk**
½ teaspoon **Truvia** or **Splenda**

1 Pour Via, yogurt, milk and sweetener into an individual blender glass and process for about 15 seconds.

2 Pour into a chilled glass and serve.

SUMMER

Summer sunshine kindles wanderlust, and Kentucky's magnificent waterways quench the thirst for adventure while offering a welcome respite from the heat and humidity. Family celebrations often accompany these summertime explorations, with food providing the flavor that underscores future memories.

The bounty of the season—tomatoes, berries, corn, eggplant, squash, green beans and peaches—takes center stage in the following recipes, and straightforward cooking methods liberate you from the kitchen. Grilled fare and bold barbecue dishes are ideal accompaniments to the sultry days of summer.

Plate up summertime adventure with fresh-from-the-garden eats and hot-off-the-grill cuisine.

Oyster-Stuffed Cherry Tomatoes

MAKES ABOUT 30 HORS D'OEUVRES

1½ pints **cherry tomatoes**

3.75-ounce can **smoked oysters**, drained

1 ripe **avocado**, peeled, pitted and cubed

5 teaspoons fresh **lime juice**

4 ounces **cream cheese**, softened

Cayenne pepper and **salt** to taste

1 Cut off the tops of the tomatoes.

2 With a small melon baller, scoop out tomatoes and discard pulp and seeds.

3 Sprinkle tomato shells with salt and let them drain inverted on paper towels.

4 Puree the oysters, avocado, lime juice, cream cheese, cayenne pepper and salt until mixture is smooth.

5 Transfer puree to a pastry bag and pipe it into the tomatoes.

6 Cover loosely on a platter and chill for at least an hour.

Avocado Dip

MAKES 1 CUP

2 ripe **avocados**, peeled
1 medium **tomato**
½ teaspoon **garlic**, chopped
½ teaspoon **cumin**
Salt and **pepper** to taste
½ teaspoon **lemon juice**

1 Finely dice the avocados and tomato and place them in a small mixing bowl.

2 Stir in the garlic, seasonings and lemon juice.

3 Serve with scoop-like chips.

Mixed Greens *with* Goat Cheese *and* Blackberry Vinaigrette

MAKES 4 SERVINGS

1 package **mixed lettuce**
1 cup **carrots**, shredded
1 cup **goat cheese**, crumbled
1 cup sweetened, **dried cranberries**
1 cup **mandarin oranges**
1 cup **walnuts**, toasted

Blackberry Vinaigrette
½ cup **olive oil**
1 teaspoon **onion**, chopped
1 tablespoon **red pepper**, chopped
⅓ cup **blackberries**
⅛ cup **rice wine vinegar** or **sherry vinegar**
⅛ teaspoon **salt**
¼ teaspoon **Dijon mustard**
1 clove **garlic**, pressed
2 teaspoons **Splenda**

1 Place greens in a large salad bowl and top with salad ingredients.

2 When ready to serve, top salad with blackberry vinaigrette.

Blackberry Vinaigrette

1 Pour 1-2 teaspoons of oil into a non-stick skillet and sauté onion and red pepper for about a minute over high heat. Remove pan from heat and allow oil mixture to cool.

2 Place berries in a food processor with the cooled onion and pepper mixture.

3 Add vinegar, salt, mustard, garlic and sweetener to berries and blend.

5 Slowly add the remaining oil and blend well.

SERVING SUGGESTION: *Position carrots, cheese, cranberries, oranges and walnuts in separate bowls around greens so that guests can assemble their salads, and then top with the vinaigrette.*

Heirloom Tomatoes *with* Green Goddess Dressing

MAKES 6-8 SERVINGS

6 to 8 **heirloom tomatoes**
Lettuce leaves

Green Goddess Dressing
½ cup **sour cream**
1 cup **mayonnaise**
3 tablespoons fresh **lemon juice**
1 clove **garlic**, chopped
1 tablespoon **anchovy paste**
⅓ cup **green onion**, chopped
⅓ cup fresh **flat-leaf parsley**, chopped
2 tablespoons fresh **tarragon** leaves, chopped
2 tablespoons fresh **chives**, chopped
Dash of **sea salt** and **black pepper**

1 Place all ingredients, except tomatoes and lettuce, in a food processor and blend until creamy and pale green.

2 Cover and chill for 8 hours before serving.

3 When ready to serve, slice tomatoes on top of lettuce leaves on individual salad plates. Pour dressing over tomatoes and serve.

Gazpacho Salad

3-ounce envelope **plain gelatin**

¼ cup cold **water**

10-ounce can **tomato soup**

8-ounce package **cream cheese**, softened

½ cup **celery**, chopped

½ cup **green pepper**, chopped

¼ cup **onion**, finely chopped

1 teaspoon **lemon juice**

¼ cup **pecans**, chopped

1 cup **mayonnaise**

4-ounce can **green chilies**, chopped

1 Mix gelatin in water and stir to dissolve.

2 Heat soup and gelatin mixture, stirring constantly.

3 Add softened cream cheese and blend.

4 Cool the mixture to room temperature and add vegetables, lemon juice, nuts, mayonnaise and chilies.

5 Pour into a 9x13-inch glass baking dish; refrigerate overnight.

6 To serve, cut in squares and place on top of lettuce leaves.

Avocado Salad

MAKES 4 SERVINGS

Red or **green leafy lettuce** leaves

4 large **avocados**, peeled

2 tablespoons **olive oil**

Red wine vinegar or dark **balsamic vinegar**, to taste

¼ cup fresh **lemon** or **lime juice**

Salt and **pepper** to taste

1 **red onion**, sliced and separated into rings

1 **tomato**

1 Wash and dry the lettuce leaves and place them on individual plates.

2 Slice the avocados in half lengthwise, remove the pits, cut into slices and fan them out over the lettuce.

3 Whisk together the olive oil, vinegar, lemon juice, salt and pepper.

4 Pour over avocado. This keeps the avocado from turning brown too quickly.

5 Place sliced red onion rings and a few tomato wedges in the middle for garnish.

Orange *and* Avocado Salad

MAKES 2 SERVINGS

1 cup **pecans**, toasted
½ teaspoon **salt**
Fresh **spinach**
1 **navel orange**
1 **avocado**, peeled and
    sliced

Vinaigrette Dressing
½ cup fresh squeezed
    orange juice
2 tablespoons **rice wine**
    vinegar
½ teaspoon **Splenda**
¼ cup **olive oil**

1 Place pecans in a skillet and toast on high for a couple of minutes, shaking the pan constantly. Lightly salt and set aside to cool.

2 Place spinach on serving dishes.

3 Peel navel orange, tear apart sections and cut sections into small chunks. Place equal amounts on each of the two serving plates.

4 Top with sliced avocado and pecans.

5 Pour a few tablespoons of dressing over salad and serve.

Vinaigrette Dressing

5 Add fresh squeezed orange juice, vinegar, sweetener and oil to a small bowl and mix well.

Honey Potato Salad

MAKES 6-8 SERVINGS

2 pounds baby **Yukon gold potatoes**, peeled
½ cup local **honey**
¼ cup **Dijon mustard**
2 tablespoons **cider vinegar**
¼ cup **olive oil**
2 tablespoons **capers**
1 small **red onion**, chopped
3 ribs **celery**, chopped
¼ cup fresh **parsley**, chopped
Salt and **pepper** to taste

1 Boil potatoes in a large pot of salted water until just tender.

2 Mix together honey, mustard, vinegar, oil, capers, onion, celery, parsley, salt and pepper in a large bowl.

3 Cut potatoes into bite-size pieces while still warm.

4 Pour honey mixture over warm potatoes, fold gently and allow the dish to sit at room temperature for an hour before serving.

Pear *and* Blueberry Salad

MAKES 2 SERVINGS

1 ripe **pear**
¾ cup fresh **blueberries**
2 cups fresh **spinach**
½ cup sliced **red pepper**
¼ cup toasted **walnuts** or
   pecans

Honey-Dijon Vinaigrette
2 tablespoons **balsamic
   vinegar**
3 tablespoons **extra-virgin
   olive oil**
1 teaspoon **Dijon mustard**
1 tablespoon **honey**
Salt and **pepper** to taste
6 **blueberries**

1 Peel and slice the pear into a large salad bowl.

2 Add the fresh blueberries, spinach, red pepper and nuts.

Honey-Dijon Vinaigrette

1 Pour the vinegar and olive oil into a bowl. Add the mustard, honey, salt and pepper and the 6 blueberries. Blend with a hand-held blender or small food processor.

2 Pour dressing over the salad. Refrigerate the excess dressing.

Apple Tuna Salad

MAKES 2-4 SERVINGS

6-ounce can **white meat tuna**, packed in water

1 large stalk **celery**, minced

4 **radishes**, minced

1 tablespoon **red onion**, minced

½ **Granny Smith apple**, minced

2 tablespoons **flat-leaf parsley**, minced

2 teaspoons **lime juice**

3 tablespoons **reduced-fat mayonnaise**

¼ cup **walnuts**, lightly toasted and minced

1 Drain the tuna and place in a bowl; flake with a fork.

2 Add the remaining ingredients and mix well. You may use more mayonnaise to taste.

3 Store in an airtight container in the refrigerator.

Three-Orange Ambrosia Salad

MAKES 4 SERVINGS

½ cup **pecans**

1 **blood orange**

1 **navel orange**

1 **tangerine** or **Valencia orange**

1 **banana**, peeled and sliced diagonally

½ cup **blackberries**

1 cup **plain yogurt**

1 teaspoon **vanilla extract**

2 tablespoons **honey**

½ cup grated **coconut**

1 Place nuts on a baking sheet and toast at 375°F for 5-8 minutes.

2 Peel oranges and slice into wheels.

3 Combine oranges, banana slices and blackberries in medium-sized bowl.

4 Combine yogurt, vanilla and honey.

5 Gently toss fruit with dressing. Cover and place in refrigerator to chill.

6 Before serving, sprinkle with coconut and toasted pecans.

Champion Chicken Spinach Strawberry Salad

MAKES 6-8 SERVINGS

¾ cup **sugar**
1 teaspoon **salt**
1 teaspoon **dry mustard**
⅓ cup **red wine vinegar**
1 teaspoon **onion juice**
1 cup **vegetable oil**
1 tablespoon **poppy seeds**
1 cup sliced **almonds**
6 cups fresh **spinach**, torn
1 quart **strawberries**, sliced
3 **kiwi**, peeled and sliced
3 cups **chicken**, cooked and chopped

1 Process the sugar, salt, dry mustard, vinegar and onion juice in a blender until smooth.

2 Turn the blender on high and add the oil in a slow stream.

3 Pour the mixture in a serving bowl and stir in poppy seeds.

4 Cover and refrigerate.

5 Place the almonds on a baking sheet and bake at 350°F for approximately 3 to 5 minutes.

6 Place spinach on plates and top with strawberries, kiwi, almonds and chicken.

7 Gently drizzle the dressing over the top.

Chutney Chicken Salad

MAKES 10 SERVINGS

6 cups cooked **chicken**, chopped

1½ cups **celery**, finely chopped

17-ounce can **apricots** in heavy syrup, drained

2 tablespoons **chutney**, preferably Major Grey's

1 cup **mayonnaise**

1 tablespoon fresh **lemon juice**

1½ teaspoons **soy sauce**

Salt and freshly ground **black pepper** to taste

1½ cups toasted **pecans**, chopped

Lettuce leaves

1 Combine the chicken and the celery.

2 In a blender or food processor, puree the drained apricots with the chutney.

3 Add the mayonnaise, lemon juice and soy sauce and mix well. Season with salt and pepper.

4 Fold the dressing into the chicken mixture.

5 Fold in the pecans or sprinkle them over each portion before serving.

6 Place portions of the chicken salad on lettuce leaves and serve.

Marinated Italian Sub

MAKES 6-8 SERVINGS

¼ cup **red wine vinegar**
1 teaspoon dried **oregano**
½ teaspoon **dry mustard**
Dash of **salt** and **pepper**
½ cup **extra-virgin olive oil**
1 loaf **Italian bread** with sesame seeds, 24" long
¼ cup **pepperoncini**, seeded and sliced
¼ cup **cherry peppers**, chopped
2 cups **lettuce**, finely chopped
4 **tomatoes**, thinly sliced
5 ounces each of **cappicola**, **salami**, **country ham**, **mortadella** and **provolone cheese**, thinly sliced

1 Combine vinegar, oregano, mustard, salt and pepper in a small bowl and stir well. Whisk in olive oil.

2 Lay out 3 long pieces of plastic wrap side by side and slightly overlapping. Cut bread lengthwise into two pieces and place on the wrap.

3 Spread the pepperoncini and cherry peppers over the bottom half. Evenly scatter the lettuce, then tomatoes.

4 Drizzle with a few tablespoons of dressing. Layer the meats and top with cheese.

5 Drizzle the remaining dressing over the cut side of the top half of the loaf and place it on the sandwich.

6 Wrap the plastic securely around it and refrigerate for at least 1 hour or up to 4 hours.

7 To serve, unwrap and slice the sandwich into pieces about 3 to 4 inches wide.

Stuffed Sweet Peppers *with* Creole Cabbage

MAKES 6 SERVINGS

Cabbage

1 small head **cabbage**

½ **green pepper**, chopped

14.5-ounce can peeled and diced **tomatoes**

Salt and **pepper** to taste

½ teaspoon **garlic salt**

2 tablespoons **brown sugar**

1 tablespoon **vinegar**

¼ cup **onion**, chopped

Stuffed Peppers

1 each **yellow**, **red** and **orange bell peppers**

3 **sweet Italian sausages**

1 cup cooked **wild rice**

¼ cup **chili sauce**

1 tablespoon **basil pesto**

Cabbage

1 Shred cabbage and place in a large mixing bowl.

2 Add green pepper, tomatoes, salt, pepper, garlic salt, brown sugar and vinegar.

3 Mix in onion and stir.

4 Pour the mixture into a 9x13-inch coated baking dish.

Stuffed Peppers

1 Slice bell peppers in half and remove seeds and membranes so peppers will sit easily in a baking dish.

2 Remove casings and cook sausage in a skillet over medium heat until crumbly and done.

3 Drain and pour into a mixing bowl.

4 Add wild rice, chili sauce and pesto. Adjust seasonings and mix well.

5 Spoon rice and sausage mixture into pepper halves and place on top of cabbage mixture in baking dish.

6 Bake at 350°F for 45 minutes.

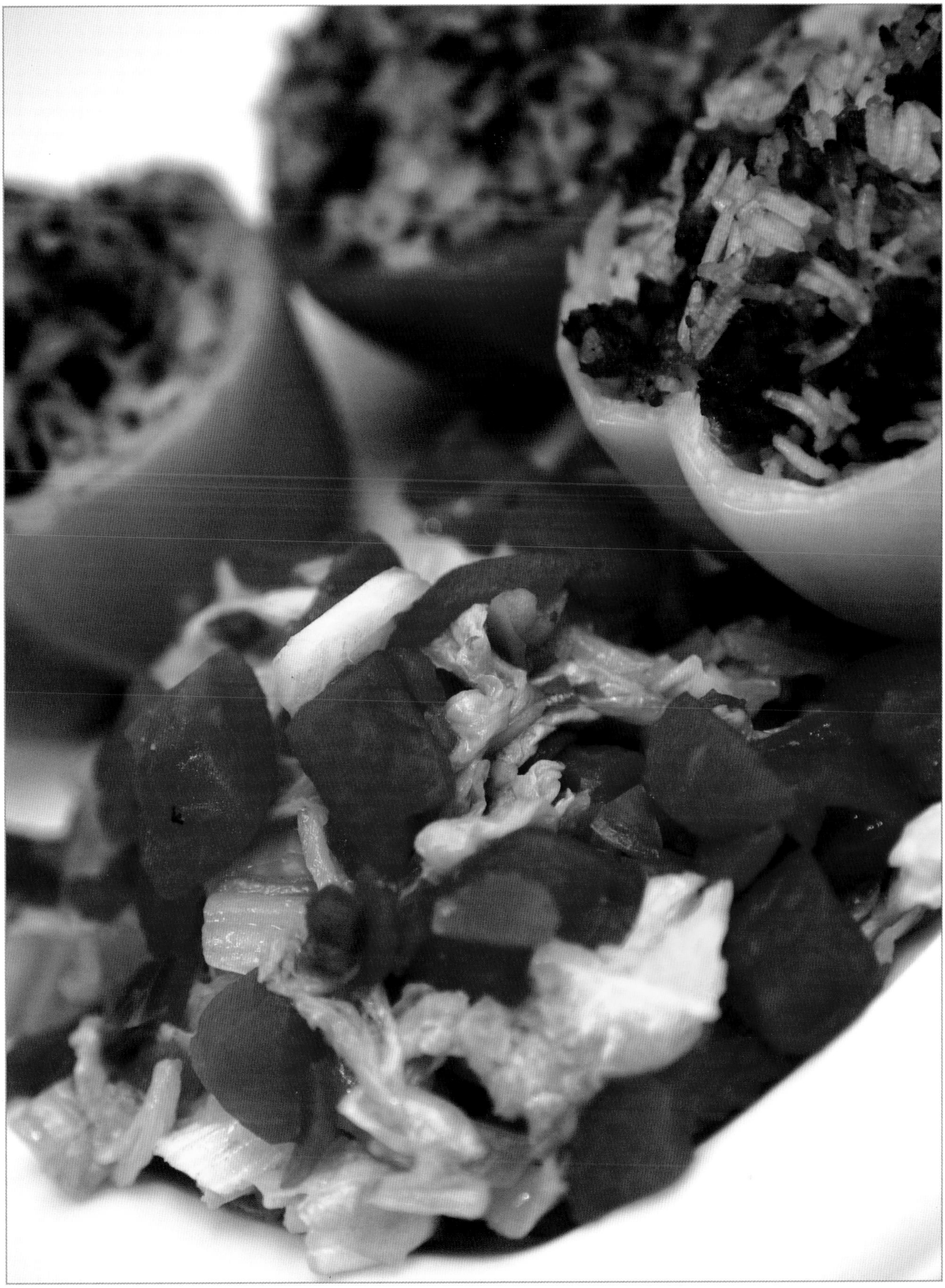

Chicken *with* Mango Salsa *and* Coconut Rice

MAKES 4 SERVINGS

4 6-ounce skinless, boneless **chicken breasts**

Sauce for Chicken
2 tablespoons low sodium **soy sauce**
¾ teaspoon **lime rind**, grated
4 teaspoons fresh **lime juice**
1 tablespoon **green onion**, chopped
1 tablespoon fresh **cilantro**, chopped
2 teaspoons fresh **ginger**, peeled and grated
1½ teaspoons **brown sugar**
1½ teaspoons **dark sesame oil**
1½ teaspoons **honey**
1 clove **garlic**, minced

1 Place chicken breasts in a large, non-stick skillet coated with cooking spray.

2 Cook over medium-high heat for about 3 minutes on each side.

3 Remove chicken from the heat, cool and cut into ¼-inch slices.

4 After chicken is cooled and sliced, return it to the pan, pour the sauce over it and cook for about 3 minutes or until done.

5 Serve the hot chicken with sauce over the rice and top it with the fresh salsa.

Sauce for Chicken

1 Place sauce ingredients in a blender and process until well mixed.

Coconut Rice
¾ cup **flaked coconut**
1 cup **jasmine rice**,
uncooked
¼ teaspoon **salt**
13.5-ounce can **light
coconut milk**

Mango Salsa
1 cup ripe **mango**, peeled
and cubed
¼ cup **red onion**, diced
¼ cup fresh **mint**,
chopped
1½ tablespoons **jalapeño
pepper**, finely chopped
and seeded

Coconut Rice
1 Place the coconut on a baking sheet. Toast it under
the broiler—watching it the entire time—turning it
constantly with a spatula, until the coconut is lightly
browned. It shrinks to about ¼ cup.

2 Combine the rice, coconut, salt and coconut milk in
a medium saucepan, cover and bring to boil over
medium-high heat, stirring once.
3 Reduce heat and simmer for 15 minutes or until the
liquid is absorbed.

4 Remove from the heat and keep covered until ready
to serve.

Mango Salsa
1 To prepare the salsa, combine the mango, onion,
mint and jalapeño pepper in a medium bowl and toss.

Grilled Bourbon Salmon

MAKES 4 SERVINGS

¼ cup **brown sugar**, packed

¼ cup Kentucky **bourbon**

¼ cup **Dijon mustard**

½ teaspoon **cayenne pepper**

¼ cup **lemon juice**

4 **salmon** fillets

Salt

1 Combine the sugar, bourbon, mustard, cayenne pepper and lemon juice in a small mixing bowl and whisk.

2 Pour mixture into a shallow dish and place fish in marinade for about 30 minutes.

3 Remove fish and discard marinade. Sprinkle fish with salt and place on a hot grill.

4 Reduce heat to medium high and cook for about 10 minutes or until fish flakes easily. Do not turn fish; do not overcook.

Plated with Squash and Tomato Casserole, the recipe for which appears on page 122.

Beef Tenderloin *with* Blackberry Sauce

MAKES 8-12 SERVINGS

10 pounds **beef tenderloin**, trimmed
Garlic olive oil
Salt to taste
Freshly cracked **black pepper** to taste

Blackberry Sauce
12-ounce bottle **chili sauce**
14-ounce bottle **ketchup**
5-ounce bottle **Worcestershire sauce**
12-ounce bottle **Indian curry sauce**
10-ounce bottle A.1. **Steak Sauce**
1 cup seedless **blackberry jam**
2 large **garlic** heads, baked
Fresh **blackberries** to garnish

1 Place tenderloin in a roasting pan, coat with oil and sprinkle with salt and pepper.

2 Roast tenderloin at 400°F until meat thermometer reads 130°F for medium rare, about 35 minutes.

3 Cool for 10 minutes and then slice.

Blackberry Sauce

1 Mix all ingredients together.

2 When ready to serve, bring to room temperature. Add fresh blackberries to garnish.

Orange Roughy *in* Tomato-Mushroom Wine Sauce

MAKES 6 SERVINGS

2 tablespoons **olive oil**

½ large **onion**, chopped

6 cloves fresh **garlic**, chopped

6 **tomatoes**, peeled and chopped

16-ounce package fresh **mushrooms**

1 to 1½ cups **dry white wine**

6 **orange roughy** fillets

Salt and **pepper** to taste

2 tablespoons **Italian seasoning**

2 teaspoons **Old Bay seasoning**

1 Sauté the onion and garlic in olive oil in a large pan.

2 Add the tomatoes and mushrooms and cook for several minutes.

3 Pour in the wine.

4 Season the fillets with salt and pepper.

5 Mix together the Italian seasoning and the Old Bay seasoning and sprinkle over fillets.

6 Place the fish in the pan with the vegetable and wine mixture and cook over low heat until the fish is opaque.

Spinach-Feta Burgers

MAKES 4 SERVINGS

10-ounce package **frozen spinach**

1 pound **ground round beef**

1-ounce package **onion soup mix**

¼ cup **feta cheese**

½ teaspoon **garlic powder**

¼ teaspoon **pepper**

1 Cook spinach and drain well.

2 Combine spinach, beef, soup mix and cheese together and mix well.

3 Shape into hamburger patties and sprinkle with garlic powder and pepper.

4 Cook over a hot grill, turning once, for desired doneness.

5 Serve on hamburger buns.

Cuban Arroz Con Pollo

MAKES 6-8 SERVINGS

6 cloves **garlic**, peeled

2 tablespoons **salt**

2 teaspoons **pepper**

¼ cup **orange juice**

¼ cup **lemon juice**

4 pounds skinned **chicken thighs**, **legs** and **breasts**

¼ cup **olive oil**

2 medium **onions**, peeled and finely chopped

1 large **green pepper**, cored, seeded and finely chopped

3 cups **chicken broth**

1 envelope **Goya Sazón seasoning packet** from a 1.41-ounce box

2 tablespoons **tomato sauce**

2 cups **short grain rice**

¼ cup **sherry** or additional chicken broth

2 eight-ounce cans **petit pois (tiny peas)**, drained

6-ounce jar **pimientos**, drained and cut into strips

1 Mash the garlic into a paste with the salt and pepper.

2 Mix in the juices and pour half the mixture over the chicken pieces.

3 Marinate in the refrigerator for about an hour.

4 Heat the oil over medium heat in a wide, shallow pan—a paella pan if possible. ·

5 Blot the chicken pieces on paper towels and discard used marinade. Brown the chicken in the hot oil.

6 In the same oil, sauté the onions and green pepper until the onions are translucent, about 3 minutes.

7 Add the broth, Sazón seasoning, tomato sauce, the remaining half of the marinade and the chicken; simmer for about 5 minutes.

8 Add the rice and stir just enough to cover it with liquid. If the rice is not fully covered, add sherry and more broth if necessary.

9 Simmer uncovered until all the liquid has been absorbed and the rice is cooked (approximately 30 minutes). Add more broth or wine if needed.

10 Remove the pan from the heat. Stir in the peas and pimientos. Let it rest for a few minutes before serving.

Best-Ever Baby Back Ribs

MAKES 2 SERVINGS PER SLAB

Slab of **pork baby back ribs** (a 12- to 18-inch slab per 2 people)
Worcestershire sauce
Paul Prudhomme's **Pork & Veal Magic** or The Pampered Chef **Smoky Barbecue Rub**
Barbecue sauce mixed with 2 tablespoons **orange marmalade**

1 Preheat the oven to 200-250°F.

2 Pour one cup of water into the bottom of a broiler pan. Place the broiler rack on top and set the pan aside.

3 Sprinkle approximately one tablespoon of Worcestershire sauce on each slab of ribs; rub it in evenly.

4 Sprinkle approximately 1½ tablespoons of Pork & Veal Magic or Smoky Barbecue Rub on both sides of each slab; rub this in evenly.

5 Place the seasoned slabs of ribs onto the broiler rack and wrap the entire pan tightly with heavy-duty aluminum foil.

6 Place in the preheated oven for about 3 hours.

7 After the ribs have steam cooked, remove them from the oven and heat the barbecue grill.

8 If adding orange marmalade to the barbecue sauce, heat the sauce to melt the marmalade fully.

9 Place the ribs on the grill and baste with the barbecue sauce. The ribs won't need to be on the grill for long, as they are already cooked. You just want to heat the ribs, slightly caramelizing the barbecue sauce.

In the May 2009 issue of Kentucky Monthly, *readers shared their favorite family recipes for a perfect Kentucky-style barbecue. The following four dishes, along with this one submitted by Candy Charters of Frankfort, are examples some of the tastiest barbecue recipes in the state.*

Fischer's Camp Barbecue

MAKES 10-12 SERVINGS

2½ to 3 pounds of lean **sirloin tip**

4 tablespoons **onion,** chopped

2 tablespoons **white or apple cider vinegar**

2 tablespoons **Worcestershire sauce**

2 tablespoons **brown sugar**

1 teaspoon **salt**

1 teaspoon **paprika**

1 teaspoon **chili powder**

½ teaspoon **pepper**

¼ teaspoon **cinnamon**

Dash of **ground cloves**

1 large can **tomato sauce**

¾ cup **water**

1 Mix all ingredients in a slow cooker.

2 Cook about 4 hours if using high heat (8 hours for low heat).

3 Remove meat from the slow cooker, and shred with two forks.

3 Serve on a bun or with corn bread.

Beth Fischer of Frankfort submitted this recipe as a tribute to the family of her husband, Steve.

Bourbon Chipotle Barbecue Sauce

MAKES 10-12 SERVINGS

1 cup **ketchup**
¼ cup **white vinegar**
¼ cup **water**
¼ cup **molasses**
¼ cup Kentucky **bourbon**
1 tablespoon **chipotle flakes** or **powder**
2 tablespoons **honey**
1 tablespoons freshly ground **pepper**

1 Combine all the ingredients in a nonstick or non-aluminum saucepan over high heat.

2 Use a whisk to blend the ingredients until smooth.

3 When the mixture comes to a boil, reduce the heat and let simmer uncovered for 30-45 minutes, stirring occasionally.

4 It is best to make the sauce a day or two before using it so the flavors can blend. Keep it tightly covered in the refrigerator and stir well before using.

TIPS: *Do not apply the sauce until the last few minutes of grilling or oven broiling, as sauce will blacken and burn quickly. Keep meat with sauce on it away from direct flame. If baking the ribs in an oven, apply the sauce sooner. However, make sure pork ribs are thoroughly cooked before applying sauce.*

Barbecue aficionado Charles Winter of Frankfort submitted this recipe, which he smothers on meat that has been prepared in his homemade bourbon-barrel smoker.

Baked Barbecue Chicken

MAKES 4 SERVINGS

1 **chicken**, cut into pieces
Garlic salt
Seasoning salt
Pepper

Sauce
1 **onion**, chopped
2 **garlic** cloves, minced
1 tablespoon **oil**
1 cup **ketchup**
¼ cup **balsamic vinegar**
3 tablespoons **brown spicy mustard**
2 tablespoons **Worcestershire sauce**
¼ cup **brown sugar**
¼ cup **chili sauce**
¾ cup **beer**

1 Dust chicken with garlic salt, seasoning salt and pepper and place in a 9x13-inch baking dish lined with foil.

2 Brush sauce over seasoned chicken pieces.

3 Bake at 350°F for one hour.

Sauce

1 Sauté onion and garlic in oil in a large saucepan over medium-high heat.

2 Add ketchup, vinegar, mustard, Worcestershire sauce, brown sugar and chili sauce.

3 Stir in beer and cook over medium-low heat for about 10 minutes.

4 Remove from heat.

Pulled Pork *with* Corn Bread

Pork butt
Equal parts:
   Garlic powder
   Onion powder
   Cajun seasoning
   Soul seasoning
   Seasoned salt
   Pepper
   Oregano
   Basil
   Thyme
   Crushed allspice
Dash of **cinnamon**

Corn Bread
2 cups **cornmeal**
2 **eggs**
Salt and **pepper** to taste
Dash of **sugar**
½ cup **oil** or **bacon grease**
Buttermilk

1 Combine all dry ingredients and rub into meat.

2 Once the pork butt has been slowly cooked in a smoker, pull the pork. This can be done using two forks to pull the meat into small sections.

Corn Bread

1 Mix cornmeal, eggs, salt, pepper, sugar and oil (or bacon grease) in a bowl with enough buttermilk to make the consistency pourable.

2 Cook corn bread on an open griddle until bubbles appear in the batter. Turn the corn bread cakes and allow to cook on the other side.

For Assembly

1 Pile the pulled pork on top of a piece of fried corn bread.

2 Cover the pork and the fried corn bread with homemade barbecue sauce.

Barbecue Sauce

1 tablespoon whole **cloves**

1 tablespoon **allspice**

1 jar **dark molasses**

2 bottles **ketchup**

Dash **cinnamon**

¾ bag **dark brown sugar**

4 tablespoons **onion flakes**

4 cloves **garlic**, crushed

2 **bay leaves**

Louisiana hot sauce to taste

Salt and **pepper** to taste

1 cup of Buffalo Trace Kentucky Straight **Bourbon**

Barbecue Sauce

1 Tie the cloves and allspice in a sachet.

2 Combine all ingredients, including clove and allspice sachet, in a saucepan.

3 Cook slowly until mixture thickens. Remove sachet once sauce is thick.

Kentucky Monthly *reader Linda Hubbard's family used to own a barbecue restaurant. She and her husband, Mike, of Lexington, swear by this recipe for pulled pork.*

Balsamic Green Beans

MAKES 4 SERVINGS

1 pound tiny **green beans**
2 tablespoons **balsamic vinegar**
1 tablespoon **brown sugar**
1 teaspoon **Dijon mustard**
2 **shallots**, minced
2 tablespoons **olive oil**
1 teaspoon **salt**
½ teaspoon **pepper**

1 Blanch green beans in boiling, salted water for 5 to 6 minutes.

2 Plunge into ice water to stop the cooking process and drain well.

3 Stir together the vinegar, sugar and mustard and set aside.

4 Cook shallots in the oil in a frying pan.

5 Stir in the salt, pepper and vinegar mixture into the pan.

6 Add the beans to the pan and toss to coat.

7 Serve immediately.

Fresh Corn Casserole

2 cups fresh **corn**

1 stick **butter**, melted

2 **eggs**

¼ cup fresh **basil**, chopped

1 cup **cheddar** or **jack cheese**, shredded

1 cup **sour cream** or **ricotta cheese**

½ cup **cornmeal**

1 Butter a 2-quart casserole.

2 Purée 1 cup of corn with butter and eggs in a blender or food processor.

3 Combine remaining ingredients in a bowl and add puréed mixture. Mix well.

4 Pour into the prepared dish and bake uncovered at 350°F for 30 to 40 minutes.

Creamed Corn

4 ears fresh **corn**, shucked
1 pint **heavy cream**
1 pinch of **salt**
1 pinch of **pepper**

1 Cut corn kernels from cobs.

2 Add all ingredients to saucepan and cook over low heat until reduced and thickened.

3 Serve immediately.

Tex-Mex Corn *on the* Cob

MAKES 4 SERVINGS

4 ears fresh **corn**, husks and silks removed
½ stick **butter**
½ teaspoon **chili powder**
¼ teaspoon **cumin**
½ teaspoon **salt**
1 teaspoon **lime juice**

1 Place corn in a large pot and cover with water.

2 Cover and bring to a boil.

3 Turn down heat and cook until tender; drain.

4 Melt butter in a small saucepan and add chili powder, cumin, salt and lime juice.

5 Pour into a small dish and serve with hot corn.

Grilled Summer Squash *and* Sweet Onion

MAKES 8 SERVINGS

4 large **yellow squash**
½ teaspoon **lemon pepper**
½ teaspoon **salt**
Cooking spray
1 large **Vidalia onion**
½ teaspoon **salt**
1 teaspoon **prepared horseradish**
1 tablespoon **mayonnaise**

1 Cut each squash in half lengthwise.

2 Spray the open sides with cooking spray and sprinkle with seasonings.

3 Place squash face down on a medium hot grill and cook for about 10 minutes.

4 Clean the onion, removing the outer skins.

5 Cut the onion in half and spray the inner sides with cooking spray.

6 Place directly on the top grill rack and cook over medium heat for 15 minutes.

7 Remove onion and cut each side in quarters.

8 Sprinkle with salt while the onion is hot.

9 Combine the horseradish and mayonnaise in a small serving bowl to use as a dip for the vegetables.

Summer Vegetable Pie

MAKES 6 SERVINGS

1 pound fresh **mushrooms**, sliced

1 **onion**, sliced

2 **zucchini** or **yellow squash**, sliced

1 **green pepper**, sliced

3 or 4 tablespoons **butter**

1 teaspoon **salt**

¼ teaspoon **black pepper**

Dash of **garlic salt**

10-inch **pie shell**

1 **tomato**, sliced

1 cup Hellman's **mayonnaise**

1 cup **mozzarella cheese**, grated

1 Bake the pie shell at 325°F for 20 minutes. Remove and cool.

2 Sauté the vegetables, except tomatoes, in butter until they are tender-crisp, but not soft.

3 Drain vegetables well and add seasonings.

4 Place tomato slices in the bottom of the pie shell.

5 Add the sautéed vegetables.

6 Mix together the mayonnaise and cheese in a small mixing bowl; cover the pie with the cheese mixture.

7 Bake uncovered at 325°F for 45 minutes to 1 hour.

Red *and* Green Coleslaw

MAKES 4 SERVINGS

½ **green cabbage**

½ **red cabbage**

1 **Gala apple**, peeled and shredded

½ teaspoon **seasoning salt**

½ teaspoon **pepper**

1 **carrot**, shredded

½ cup **green pepper**, chopped

½ cup **mayonnaise**

1 Shred the cabbage and mix with the apple in a large mixing bowl.

2 Season with salt and pepper.

3 Add carrot and green pepper.

4 Stir in mayonnaise and mix well.

5 Cover and refrigerate until ready to use.

Asian Marinated Asparagus

MAKES 8 SERVINGS

3 to 4 pounds **asparagus**, blanched
1 cup **soy sauce**
1 cup **sugar**
1 cup **white wine vinegar**
Sesame seeds, toasted
Sweet red pepper, chopped, for garnish

1 Mix together soy sauce, sugar and white wine vinegar.

2 Heat the mixture in a saucepan over medium heat, stirring until sugar has dissolved.

3 Cool sauce and pour over cooled, blanched asparagus.

4 Marinate for 4 to 6 hours.

5 Drain and place on serving tray.

6 To serve, top with toasted sesame seeds and chopped, sweet red pepper for color.

To Blanch Asparagus

1 Bring a large pot of water to a boil.

2 Place asparagus in the boiling water for 3 minutes, then remove and immediately plunge in ice-cold water to stop the cooking process; drain.

Asparagus *with* Lemon Zest

1 pound fresh **asparagus**, trimmed

2 teaspoons **lemon zest**

½ teaspoon **salt**

¼ teaspoon **pepper**

1 tablespoon **butter**

1 tablespoon **soy sauce**

1 Cook asparagus in a covered saucepan with 1 inch of water for about 7 minutes, or until tender.

2 Drain and return to the pan; add lemon zest, salt, pepper, butter and soy sauce.

3 Shake pan to coat all.

Eggplant Stacks

MAKES 6-8 SERVINGS

1 large **eggplant**, peeled
½ cup **cornmeal mix**
½ cup **flour**
1 tablespoon **sea salt** plus
sea salt for soaking
eggplant
Pepper to taste
2 **eggs**, beaten
1 large **onion**, sliced
3 cups prepared **marinara sauce**
1 cup **goat cheese**, crumbled
2 cups **mozzarella cheese**
½ cup **red wine**
Cooking oil

1 Slice eggplant in quarter-inch slices and place in a bowl of water to which salt has been added.

2 Soak for 20 minutes and drain.

3 Mix together cornmeal and flour; add salt and pepper.

4 Pour ½-inch cooking oil in a large frying pan and heat on medium high.

5 Dip eggplant slices into the beaten eggs and coat with the cornmeal mixture.

6 Place the slices in the hot oil and cook each side until golden brown. Drain each slice.

7 Coat a baking dish with cooking spray.

8 Place the largest eggplant slice on the bottom of dish, top with a spoonful of marinara sauce, goat cheese, rings of onion and mozzarella.

9 Place another round of eggplant on top and repeat layering.

10 Make each stack 3-4 slices tall, finishing the top with sauce.

11 Pour the wine over all and bake uncovered in a 350°F oven for 30-45 minutes, until cheese is melted and the sauce is bubbling.

Squash *and* Tomato Casserole

MAKES 6 SERVINGS

1 small **onion**, chopped

½ **red pepper**, chopped

1 tablespoon **olive oil**

2 cups **squash**, cooked

10.75-ounce can **cream of chicken soup**

10-ounce can **tomatoes with green chiles**

1 cup **cheddar cheese**, shredded

3 tablespoons **flour**

⅓ cup **butter**, melted

2 cups **seasoned croutons**

2 tablespoons **butter**, melted

1 Sauté onion and pepper in olive oil.

2 Combine this mixture with the squash, soup, tomatoes, cheese and flour.

3 Mix well and pour into a greased 2-quart baking dish.

4 Top with croutons and drizzle topping with melted butter.

5 Bake at 350°F for about 35 minutes or until bubbly.

See page 93 for photo.

Green Beans *with* Caramelized Onions *and* Bacon

MAKES 4 SERVINGS

1 pound fresh **green beans**

½ pound **bacon**

1 large **onion**, sliced into rings

1 clove **garlic**, minced

Salt and **pepper** to taste

1 Fry bacon in a large skillet until crisp; drain, break into pieces and set aside.

2 Pour off excess bacon drippings and sauté onion rings in about 1 tablespoon of the grease, or use olive oil.

3 Cook onions, stirring constantly, over medium heat until the onions turn a rich, golden brown. When the onions are almost finished, add garlic. Remove from pan and set aside.

4 Pour 1 tablespoon olive oil or grease back into the skillet. Pinch off the ends of the green beans and sauté for 8 to 10 minutes. They should remain crunchy but still cooked through.

5 Remove from the heat and pour into a serving bowl, top with onions and sprinkle with the bacon.

Chocolate Berry Tart

MAKES 8 SERVINGS

18-ounce roll refrigerated **chocolate chip cookie dough**
8 ounces **cream cheese**
⅛ cup **sugar**
1 teaspoon **vanilla extract**
11-ounce package fresh **blueberries**
3 cups sliced **strawberries**
½ cup **raspberry jam**
2 tablespoons **water**

1 Slice cookie dough into rounds and place on a 12-inch pizza pan, flattening dough with your fingers so that all the pan is covered. Or, arrange dough in a circle on a cookie sheet and flatten to make the circle even.

2 Bake at 350°F for about 10 minutes, or until cookie begins to turn brown.

3 Remove from oven and cool.

4 Place cream cheese in a food processor and mix until smooth.

5 Add vanilla and sugar and mix well.

6 Spread cheese mixture over cookie dough to within ½ inch of the edge.

7 Using a knife, lightly draw sections through the cheese to indicate portions where berries will be placed. Do not cut through the cookie.

8 Place blueberries in one section, layer strawberries in another until the entire cookie is covered with red and blue.

9 Heat the jam and stir in water to make a thin syrup.

10 Drizzle the syrup over the entire cookie.

11 Cut cookie with a knife or pizza wheel to serve.

Crème *de* Menthe Mousse

MAKES 6 SERVINGS

16 large **marshmallows**
⅔ cup **green crème de menthe**
2 cups **whipping cream**
Fresh **strawberries**
Shaved **chocolate**

1 Place the marshmallows and crème de menthe in the top of a double boiler.

2 Cook and stir over medium-high heat until the marshmallows have melted; cool well.

3 Whip cream and fold into the melted mixture.

4 Pour the mixture into a mold and refrigerate at a very cold temperature for at least 3 hours—overnight is best.

5 When ready to serve, garnish with strawberries and shaved chocolate.

Kentucky Cold Brown

MAKES 12 SERVINGS

1 loaf **angel food cake**

1 8-ounce tub
  mascarpone cheese,
  room temperature

½ cup **sugar**

Flavored liqueur to taste
  like Bailey's Irish Cream,
  Kahlua, or Amarula Fruit
  Cream Liqueur
  recommended

½ bar **dark chocolate**

1 quart **strawberries**

1 tin chocolate
  Pepperidge Farm
  pirouette cookies

1 Mix mascarpone, sugar and liqueur until smooth.

2 Grate dark chocolate—a mandolin grater works well—and fold into mixture.

3 Spoon sauce generously over 2 slices of angel food cake.

4 Slice 2-3 strawberries to resemble tomato slices and place on top.

5 Top with 2 pirouette cookies to resemble bacon.

6 Serve immediately. Sauce may be refrigerated for several days.

Submitted by Amandalin Ryan of Danville on behalf of Adam Johnson for the October 2011 Readers' Issue of Kentucky Monthly.

Pears *in* White Zinfandel

MAKES 8 SERVINGS

8 **pears**
2 cups **white Zinfandel**
2 tablespoons **lemon juice**
1 cup **sugar**
2 teaspoons **cinnamon**
Zest of 1 **lemon**
1 teaspoon **vanilla extract**
Créme fraiche
Mint leaves

1 Peel pears and then core from the bottom up, leaving the stems intact. Set aside.

2 In a deep saucepan, combine wine, lemon juice, sugar, cinnamon, lemon zest and vanilla extract. Bring to a boil.

3 Add the pears to the saucepan with stems up and scoop spoonfuls of liquid over them. Simmer until pears are tender, 10 to 20 minutes.

4 Remove pears and place in individual serving dishes.

5 Strain the cooking liquid and boil until reduced by half.

6 Pour wine sauce over pears and let cool.

7 Serve with créme fraiche on the side and garnish with mint leaves.

Kentucky Bourbon Sauce

MAKES 6 CUPS

1 cup **brown sugar**

1 cup granulated **sugar**

1 cup **water**

1 **lemon**, juiced and zested (approximately ¼ cup juice)

1 **orange**, zested, to taste

1 cup WindStone Farms Kentucky **strawberry jam**

1 cup **pecans**

½ to 1 cup Kentucky **bourbon**

1 Cook the first three ingredients in a saucepan until sugars are completely dissolved.

2 Remove from heat.

3 Grate the rind of the orange and lemon and add to mixture.

4 Add strawberry jam, lemon juice, pecans and bourbon.

5 Warm before serving over pound cake or ice cream.

Winner in the Dessert category in Kentucky Monthly's 2010 Recipe Contest, this recipe was submitted by Denise Scaringi of Lakeside Park.

Chocolate Espresso Cookies

MAKES 3 DOZEN

3 cups self-rising **flour**

⅔ cup unsweetened **Hershey's Special Dark cocoa powder**

½ teaspoon **espresso powder**

1 cup **unsalted butter**, room temperature

1½ cups **sugar**

2 **eggs**

1½ teaspoons **vanilla extract**

1 In a large bowl, sift together flour, cocoa powder and espresso powder. Set aside.

2 Cream butter and sugar with an electric mixer on medium speed until light and fluffy.

3 Add eggs, one at a time, beating well after each addition.

4 Add vanilla and beat. Reduce the speed to low and gradually add the flour mixture, mixing until combined and smooth.

5 Divide the dough in half, roll into a log and wrap in plastic wrap.

6 Chill in the refrigerator for an hour.

7 Preheat oven to 350°F.

8 Line baking sheets with parchment paper; set aside.

9 Slice the chilled dough and transfer cookies to baking sheets.

10 Bake for 8 to 10 minutes, until the edges are firm and the centers are slightly puffed.

11 Let cool on baking sheet for several minutes, and then transfer to a wire rack to cool completely.

12 Cookies may be frosted, dusted with powdered sugar or eaten naked!

Cherry Trifle

MAKES 8-10 SERVINGS

19.8-ounce package **fudge brownie mix**

21 ounces **cherry pie filling**

2 1-ounce packages **sugar-free white chocolate instant pudding mix**

8 ounces **whipped topping**

Dark chocolate candy bar for garnish

1 Spray a 9x13-inch glass baking dish.

2 Follow directions on box of brownie mix and bake, being careful not to overbake as brownies can become too dry.

3 Mix instant pudding according to package directions and refrigerate.

4 When brownies have cooled, break into pieces.

5 Place ½ the crumbled brownie mixture on the bottom of a large glass bowl or trifle bowl.

6 Layer with ½ the cherry pie filling and top with ½ the white chocolate pudding mixture.

7 Finish with ½ of the whipped topping and then repeat the process.

8 Garnish with grated dark chocolate.

Summertime Banana Pudding

2 3-ounce packages **vanilla instant pudding**

14-ounce can **sweetened condensed milk**

11-ounce box **vanilla wafers**

6 **bananas**, sliced

8-ounce container **whipped topping**

Cherries for garnish

1 Prepare the pudding according to package directions.

2 Add the sweetened condensed milk to the pudding and mix well.

3 In a large serving bowl, layer the vanilla wafers, bananas, pudding mixture and whipped topping; repeat layers.

4 Garnish with a few slices of banana that have been dipped in lemon juice to prevent browning.

5 Add some cherries for color.

6 Refrigerate until ready to serve.

TIP: *Forget the bowl! Get creative and layer the crust and pudding for a spin on a classic recipe.*

Summertime Peach Pie

MAKES 8 SERVINGS

3 to 4 large, fresh
peaches, peeled, sliced
¼ cup **brown sugar**
1½ cups crushed
gingersnap cookies
4 tablespoons **butter**,
melted
1 cup **sugar**
8 ounces **cream cheese**,
room temperature
8 ounces **whipped
topping**, room
temperature

1 Place sliced peaches in a bowl, sprinkle with the brown sugar and turn to coat.

2 Allow peaches to sit.

3 Combine cookies and butter and mix well.

3 Pat into the bottom of a 9-inch pie dish and bake at 350°F for about 12 minutes.

4 Remove from oven and cool.

5 Combine sugar and cream cheese in a food processor and mix well.

6 Add whipped topping and pulse until mixed.

7 Pour peaches into the crust and cover with the cream cheese mixture.

8 Spread evenly, cover and refrigerate overnight.

Peach *and* Strawberry Pie

MAKES 12 SERVINGS

1 package **cream cheese**, softened
¼ cup **sugar**
1 tablespoon **milk**
2 teaspoons **lemon juice**
9-inch **graham cracker crust**
3 cups fresh **peaches**, peeled and sliced
3 cups fresh **strawberries**, sliced

Strawberry Glaze
1 cup granulated **sugar**
2 tablespoons dry **strawberry gelatin**
2 tablespoons **cornstarch**
1 cup cold **water**

1 In a mixing bowl, beat cream cheese, sugar and milk until smooth.

2 Spread mixture over the bottom and up the sides of the pie crust.

3 Arrange peach slices over the cream cheese mixture; top with sliced stawberries.

4 Spoon the strawberry glaze mixture over the peaches.

5 Drizzle with lemon juice.

6 Refrigerate for up to 4 hours before serving with vanilla ice cream or fresh whipped cream.

Strawberry Glaze

1 Combine granulated sugar, gelatin and cornstarch in a 2-quart saucepan.

2 Gradually add cold water, stirring until combined.

3 Place over medium heat and bring to a boil. Stir and boil for 1-2 minutes, until thickened and remove from the heat.

Submitted by Kentucky Monthly reader Connie Hervey of Alexandria as a dessert to accompany the barbecue recipes in the May 2009 issue.

Summer Fruit Crisp

MAKES 6 SERVINGS

6 fresh **peaches**
½ cup **blueberries**
½ cup **raspberries**
½ cup granulated **sugar**
¼ cup **flour**
2 teaspoons **lemon zest**, grated
1 tablespoon **lemon juice**
1 tablespoon **white rum**

Crumb Topping
1½ cups **flour**
2 sticks **butter** (not softened)
½ cup granulated **sugar**
½ cup **brown sugar**
1 cup chopped **pecans** or **walnuts**

1 Peel peaches, slice and place in a bowl.

2 Add blueberries and raspberries to the sliced peaches.

3 Cover fruit with sugar, flour, lemon zest, lemon juice and rum and gently mix.

4 Set aside to allow the fruit to "juice up" while mixing the topping.

5 Place the fruit mixture in the bottom of a 8x8-inch baking dish.

6 Spread crumb mixture over fruit and bake at 350°F for 40 minutes.

7 Serve with vanilla ice cream.

Crumb Topping

1 Cut flour and butter together with pastry blender or fork.

2 Add sugars and nuts and toss, combining well.

Silky Sunshine Cocktail

MAKES 1 SERVING

1½ ounces Woodford
    Reserve **bourbon**
2 ounces **orange juice**
2 ounces **piña colada mix**
1 teaspoon **simple syrup**
Crushed ice
Orange slice, *optional*

1 Pour the liquids into a cocktail shaker and shake well.

2 Pour over ice and garnish with an orange slice.

TIP: *To make simple syrup, mix equal parts of sugar and water until sugar is thoroughly dissolved.*

FALL

As the temperature begins to cool and colorful leaves cascade from their branches, our appetite for heartier fare returns. Events across the state celebrate the harvest, and Kentuckians capitalize on the remaining days of outdoor enjoyment with treks through the autumn splendor.

Colonel's Burgoo, Potato-Curry Soup and Mushroom Chicken Chowder bring warmth to the increasingly chilly days of fall, and bourbon transitions from the glass to the plate, providing richness and depth to dishes. Our autumn recipe collection offers inventive as well as tried-and-true interpretations of Thanksgiving favorites.

Give thanks for the beauty of autumn, the flavorful food that accompanies it, and the family and friends with whom to share it.

Spicy Pecans

MAKES 16 SERVINGS

½ stick **butter**

2 tablespoons **Worcestershire sauce**

1 teaspoon **salt**

½ teaspoon **cinnamon**

⅛ teaspoon **cloves**

¼ teaspoon **garlic powder**

¼ teaspoon **cayenne pepper**

¼ teaspoon **Tabasco sauce**

4 cups **pecan halves**

1 Melt butter in a skillet.

2 Stir the remaining ingredients, with the exception of the pecans, into the butter and mix well.

3 Add the pecans and stir until well coated.

4 Place the pecans in a single layer on an ungreased baking sheet.

5 Toast pecans at 300°F for 25 to 30 minutes, stirring frequently.

Seafood Toasts

MAKES 48 PIECES

1 cup **shrimp,** cooked and chopped

½ cup **mayonnaise**

1 tablespoon **Dijon mustard**

1 cup grated **Swiss cheese**

2 teaspoons **curry powder**

1 can **water chestnuts**, drained and chopped

¼ cup **scallions**, chopped

2 twenty-four-inch **baguettes**, sliced, buttered and toasted

1 Combine the shrimp, mayonnaise, mustard, cheese, curry powder, water chestnuts and scallions.

2 Spoon 1 tablespoon of the filling on each slice of the toasted baguette.

3 Bake at 400°F until golden brown, about 10 minutes.

Austin's Inn Place Spinach Parmesan Clusters

MAKES 50 CLUSTERS

20 ounces frozen, chopped **spinach**, thawed

2 cups **herb-seasoned stuffing mix**

2 small **yellow onions**, finely chopped

6 large **eggs**, beaten

½ cup **water chestnuts**, finely chopped

¾ cup **butter**, melted

1 cup **Parmesan cheese**, grated

1 tablespoon **garlic salt**

1 tablespoon **seasoning salt**

½ teaspoon dried **thyme**

½ teaspoon **black pepper**

10 dashes **Tabasco sauce**

1 Cook spinach according to package directions, cool and drain.

2 Squeeze out excess moisture and combine with the remaining ingredients in a mixing bowl.

3 Shape into 1-inch balls and place on a baking sheet lined with parchment paper.

4 Bake at 350°F for 20 minutes.

From Austin's Inn Place bed & breakfast in Old Louisville.

Rosemary Focaccia Bread

MAKES 2 LARGE LOAVES

2 1-pound **loaves white bread dough**, frozen

1 teaspoon dried **rosemary** leaves or 1 tablespoon **Italian seasoning mix**

Fresh **Parmesan cheese**, *optional*

1 Thaw bread until workable.

2 Sprinkle with rosemary and knead on a floured space to incorporate the seasoning.

3 Form into 2 bread rounds and let the dough rise on a coated baking sheet.

4 Bake at 350°F until golden brown.

5 Freshly grated Parmesan cheese may be added the last 5 minutes of baking. Serve warm.

Favorite Corn Bread Recipe

MAKES 6 SERVINGS

1 stick **butter**

8 ounces **sour cream**

8 ounces **cream-style corn**

2 **eggs**, beaten

1 cup self-rising **cornmeal**

1 Melt the butter in an iron 9-inch skillet or baking dish.

2 Stir the sour cream into the skillet.

3 Add the corn and eggs and mix well.

4 Stir in cornmeal and place the skillet into the oven.

5 Bake at 400°F for about 25 minutes.

Best Clam Chowder Recipe

MAKES 12-14 SERVINGS

1 stick **margarine**

1 **onion**, chopped

3 10.5-ounce cans **New England clam chowder**

5 10.5-ounce cans **cream of potato soup**

2 to 4 6.5-ounce cans **clams**, minced

2 quarts **half & half**

1 Sauté the onions in margarine.

2 Add the onion mixture to the other ingredients and place in a large stockpot.

3 Bring ingredients to a boil, stirring constantly.

4 Reduce heat to low and simmer for 30 minutes.

From Lexington's Cynthia Lewis Jones, who says, "Everyone thinks the chowder is homemade, and I don't tell them any differently."

Easy French Onion Soup

MAKES 4 SERVINGS

4 **onions**
3 tablespoons **butter**
6 cups **water**
6 **beef bouillon cubes**
1¼ teaspoons
  Worcestershire sauce
½ teaspoon **salt**
⅛ teaspoon **pepper**
Leftover **French bread**,
  toast or roll
Mozzarella cheese,
  shredded

1 Peel and slice the onions and brown them in butter in a large saucepan.

2 Add the water, bouillon cubes, Worcestershire sauce and seasonings.

3 Simmer for 30 to 45 minutes.

4 Pour the soup into 4 individual, ovenproof bowls placed on a baking sheet.

5 Cut the bread into rounds and place on top of the soup.

6 Top the bread with the cheese.

7 Slide into the oven and broil until cheese melts.

TIP: *Stale, dry bread works best for topping this soup.*

Colonel's Burgoo

MAKES 12-18 SERVINGS

1 whole deep fryer **hen** (chicken)
1 medium **chuck roast** (venison)
4 **lamb chops**
2 cups **water**
1 package **kielbasa** or **smoked sausage**
1½ cups **celery**, chopped
2 cloves **garlic**, minced
14-ounce can **chicken broth**
1½ 12-cup pots strong **coffee**
2 **potatoes**, boiled, peeled and quartered
1 can **black-eyed peas**
1½ teaspoons **pepper**
1 large bag **frozen mixed vegetables** (no okra)
2 **bay leaves**
8-ounce can **tomato paste**
3 stalks **green onion**, diced

1 Place the hen, chuck roast and lamb into an open Dutch oven at 375°F. Allow the flavors to marry in the heat for 15 minutes or until seared. (The hen's skin will have formed a sealed crust.)

2 Turn the heat back to 275°F, add the water and place the lid on the Dutch oven for 45 minutes.

3 Cook the sausage, celery and garlic in a skillet until done.

4 Slice the sausage into small cubes.

5 Remove the hen, the chuck roast and the lamb from the oven and pick the meat off the bones by hand.

6 Place the meat back into the Dutch oven.

7 Add the sausage mixture and any drippings into the Dutch oven.

8 Add chicken broth, coffee, potatoes, black-eyed peas, pepper, vegetables, bay leaves and tomato paste to the meats in the Dutch oven.

9 Cover and simmer for 45 minutes, stirring frequently to obtain consistency of a stew.

10 Top with green onions to serve.

Carrollton native Jason Deatherage says his friend, Shane Broussard of Breaux Bridge, La., swapped a family recipe for Cajun gumbo for this savory burgoo recipe.

Mushroom Chicken Chowder

MAKES 8 SERVINGS

1 small **onion**, diced

3 ribs **celery** with tops, diced

½ cup **carrot**, shredded

1 clove **garlic**, minced

6 cups **chicken broth**

2 pounds **mushrooms**, sliced

2 to 3 medium **leeks**, white and the tender green tops, sliced

½ cup **red bell pepper**, chopped

3 tablespoons **butter**

1 teaspoon **lemon juice**

4 cups **chicken breasts**, cooked and diced

6.20-ounce box Uncle Ben's Original **Long Grain & Wild Rice**

1 cup **heavy cream**

Pinch of **nutmeg**

½ cup **parsley**, chopped

Salt and fresh **pepper** to taste

1 Place onion, celery, carrots, garlic and chicken broth in a large stockpot.

2 Bring mixture to a boil, reduce heat and simmer for 30 to 45 minutes.

3 Sauté the mushrooms, leeks and red pepper in butter in a saucepan over medium heat until soft.

4 Remove the mixture from the heat and add the lemon juice.

5 Combine the chicken, mushroom mixture and box of rice with the vegetable mixture and broth; simmer for about 20 minutes.

6 Before serving, add the cream, nutmeg, salt and pepper. Heat just until it boils.

7 Garnish with fresh parsley, salt and pepper.

Captain Bristol's Potato Soup

MAKES 6 SERVINGS

4 large Idaho or russet **baking potatoes**

2 white or yellow **onions**, diced

1-pound package **maple-flavored bacon**

Butter, butter substitute or extra-virgin olive oil

1 quart **fat-free chicken stock**

Freshly ground **pepper**

1 Wash and dry the potatoes; prick with a fork and bake them in a 400°F oven for one hour.

2 Allow the potatoes to cool so that the flesh becomes firm and they can be cut into cubes, skin and all.

3 Cut the bacon strips into 1-inch pieces and fry in a large skillet to desired doneness. Remove the bacon from the pan and place on a paper towel to drain.

4 Place butter in a large pot, add the onions and cook over moderate heat until the onions are translucent.

5 Add the cooked bacon, potatoes and freshly ground pepper to the onions.

6 Pour in the chicken stock. Bring the mixture to a boil and then cook on moderate heat for 30 minutes or more, stirring occasionally.

7 Turn off the heat and place a lid securely on the pan to contain moisture. Allow the soup to gradually cool down.

8 With an hand blender or potato masher, mash the potatoes or puree to desired thickness of potato.

9 Pour mixture into a covered container and chill overnight.

10 When ready to serve, slowly heat the soup in a heavy pot or slow cooker on low. Adjust seasonings and serve with crusty bread and a hearty salad.

Nonnie's Potato-Curry Soup

MAKES 10-12 SERVINGS

5 large **potatoes**
6 to 7 cups **water**
1½ teaspoons **sea salt**
¾ teaspoon **pepper**
1 to 2 tablespoons **curry**
3 tablespoons **butter**
2 to 3 cups **half & half**
2 cups **country ham bits**, cooked
2 cups **cheddar cheese**, shredded

1 Peel the potatoes or leave on skins, if preferred.

2 Cut the potatoes into chunks and cover with the water.

3 Cook in a saucepan until two-thirds tender.

4 Add the dry seasonings, adding more or less to taste.

5 Cook 5 additional minutes.

6 Using a potato masher, mash the potatoes in the pot.

7 Add the butter and half & half, stirring well.

8 Add the ham bits, cover the pot and reduce the heat to low.

9 Continue to cook 10-20 minutes.

10 Sprinkle the shredded cheese on top and serve.

Submitted to the October 2011 Readers' Issue of Kentucky Monthly *by Connie Schuermeyer of Lexington.*

Roasted Root Vegetables *with* Bourbon Molasses Vinaigrette

MAKES 8-10 SERVINGS

2 medium **red potatoes**
2 medium **carrots**
1 large **turnip**
1 medium **rutabaga**
3 tablespoons **olive oil**
3 tablespoons **canola oil**
½ teaspoon **kosher salt**
½ teaspoon **black pepper**, cracked
2 large heads **Bibb lettuce**
Asiago cheese, *optional*

Bourbon Molasses Vinaigrette
4 large cloves **garlic**
2 tablespoons **spicy brown mustard**
6 tablespoons **molasses**
3 tablespoons Kentucky **bourbon**
3 tablespoons **apple cider vinegar**
1 teaspoon **kosher salt**
¼ teaspoon **white pepper**, ground
Juice of one **lemon**
½ cup **extra-virgin olive oil**

1 Preheat the oven to 450°F.

2 Wash and peel the potatoes, carrots, turnip and rutabaga and cut the vegetables into 1-inch pieces.

3 Combine the vegetables in a bowl and toss with the oils, salt and pepper.

4 Once the vegetables are coated, turn them out onto a baking sheet and roast in the oven for 15 minutes or until the vegetables are golden brown.

5 Remove from the oven and let cool slightly.

6 To assemble the salad, wash and dry the lettuce and arrange on a large serving platter.

7 Add the roasted vegetables and drizzle with the bourbon molasses vinaigrette.

8 Garnish with slivers of Asiago cheese if desired.

Bourbon Molasses Vinaigrette

1 In a blender, puree the garlic, mustard, molasses, bourbon, vinegar, salt, pepper and lemon juice.

2 Once the mixture is totally smooth, drizzle in the olive oil while still blending to emulsify the dressing.

Shredded Carrot Salad *with* Raspberry Vinaigrette

MAKES 4 SERVINGS

5 large **carrots**

1 cup Ken's **Lite Raspberry Walnut Vinaigrette**

12 **cherry tomatoes**, halved

Fresh salad greens, **spinach** or **lettuce**

1 Grate freshly washed carrots and place in a small mixing bowl.

2 Pour vinaigrette over carrots and marinate for at least an hour.

3 Drain carrots.

4 Place tomato halves, cut sides down, in the marinade for just a few minutes, then toss tomatoes, carrots and lettuce. Or place scoops of grated carrots on top of a bed of salad greens and garnish with tomato halves.

5 No additional dressing is needed.

Cranberry Salad *with* Grapes *and* Apples

MAKES 8 SERVINGS

2 cups raw **cranberries**, ground

3 cups **miniature marshmallows**

¾ cup **sugar**

2 Granny Smith **apples**, unpeeled and diced

1 cup seedless red **grapes**, sliced

½ cup toasted **pecans**, chopped

Pinch of **salt**

8-ounce container **non-dairy whipped topping**

1 Combine cranberries, marshmallows and sugar.

2 Cover and chill overnight.

3 Add apples, grapes, pecans and salt.

4 Fold together gently with whipped topping, cover and chill.

Scrambled Eggs Alfredo *with* Country Ham *and* Asparagus

MAKES 4 SERVINGS

4 **English muffins**, split,
   toasted and buttered
10 **eggs**, beaten
¼ cup **milk** or **cream**
Salt and **pepper** to taste
2 tablespoons **butter**
8 slices **country ham**
1 pound **asparagus**
   spears, blanched or
   roasted
Chives, snipped

Easy Alfredo Sauce
½ cup **butter**
½ cup **heavy whipping**
   cream
¾ cup **Parmesan cheese**,
   grated
½ teaspoon **salt**
Dash of **pepper**

1 Preheat broiler.

2 Melt butter in a large skillet over medium heat.

3 In large bowl, beat eggs with milk or cream. Add eggs to skillet and stir while cooking until eggs are set but still fluffy.

4 Place English muffins on a broiler pan and add a spoonful of Alfredo sauce on each. Top with country ham. Divide eggs among muffins and top with the remaining Alfredo sauce.

5 Broil 6 inches from heat source for 2-3 minutes until bubbly.

6 Garnish with snipped chives and asparagus on the side. Serve immediately.

Easy Alfredo Sauce

1 Heat butter and whipping cream in a 2-quart saucepan over low heat, stirring constantly.

2 Stir in cheese, salt and pepper and continue stirring until smooth.

Norma Laufer's Boeuf Bourguignon

MAKES 10-12 SERVINGS

1 tablespoon **olive oil**

8 ounces **bacon**, diced

1½ pounds **chuck roast**, cut into 1-inch cubes

1 pound baby **carrots**

2 yellow **onions**, chopped

1 tablespoon **kosher salt**

2 teaspoons black **pepper**

2 teaspoons **garlic**, minced

½ cup **brandy**

1 bottle **dry red wine**

2½ cups **beef stock**

1 tablespoon **tomato paste**

1 teaspoon fresh **thyme** leaves

4 tablespoons **unsalted butter**, room temperature

3 tablespoons all-purpose **flour**

1 pound frozen **pearl onions**

1 pound **button mushrooms**, thickly sliced

1 Heat the olive oil in a large Dutch oven over medium heat.

2 Add the bacon and cook until the bacon is lightly browned.

3 Remove the bacon with a slotted spoon to a large plate.

4 Pat the chuck cubes dry and sprinkle with salt and pepper.

5 Sear the beef in the hot oil for 5 minutes, turning to brown on all sides.

6 Remove beef to the plate with the bacon and set aside.

7 Add the carrots, chopped onions, salt and pepper to the pan and cook for 10 minutes, stirring occasionally.

8 Add the garlic and cook for 1 minute; pour in the brandy and return the meat and bacon with juice to the pan.

9 Add the wine, beef stock, tomato paste and thyme and bring to a boil.

10 Cover and bake for 1¼ hours at 250°F, or until the meat and vegetables are very tender.

11 Remove from the oven and place on top of the stove.

12 Use a fork to combine 2 tablespoons of the butter with the flour and stir the mixture into the stew, along with the pearl onions.

13 In a separate pan, brown the mushrooms in the remaining 2 tablespoons of butter. Add to the stew.

14 Bring the stew to a boil, reduce the heat and simmer for 15 minutes.

15 Adjust the seasonings as needed and serve with toasted slices of country bread.

Norma Laufer owns the Carson House in Old Louisville with her husband, Bob.

Stuffed Pork Loin *with* Italian Sausage *and* Spinach

MAKES 8-10 SERVINGS

4- to 5-pound boneless **pork loin** (not tenderloin)

¾ pound **Italian sausage**, casings removed

10 ounces frozen chopped **spinach**, thawed

1 cup dry **herb-stuffing mix**

1 **egg**, beaten

Salt, pepper and **Italian herbs**, to taste

1 cup **white wine**

Cornstarch or **flour**

Parmesan cheese, grated

1 Cook the sausage, breaking it up as it cooks.

2 Thoroughly squeeze the spinach dry; add spinach and sausage to the stuffing mix.

3 Add the egg and mix well.

4 Butterfly the pork loin and cut 3 or 4 slits on each side, about 1 inch deep.

5 Place at least 2 pieces of string in the bottom of a baking pan, and then place the bottom loin over the string.

6 Fill the slits with the stuffing mixture, and then pack the stuffing gently on the bottom loin.

7 Place the top loin portion in position to cover the stuffing.

8 Tightly tie the string to secure the top and the bottom together or roll up the stuffed meat and tie together.

9 Sprinkle the meat with salt, pepper and herbs.

10 Pour the wine into the pan and place the pan in a 400°F oven for 30 minutes, until the wine has evaporated.

11 Add 2 cups of water and cover with foil.

12 Reduce the heat to 350°F and continue to cook for 45 to 60 minutes.

13 Add water and cornstarch or flour to the pan drippings to make 2 cups of sauce.

13 Remove the string and cut into 1-inch slices.

14 Drizzle sauce over the meat and sprinkle with grated Parmesan cheese.

Chicken, Broccoli *and* Sun-Dried Tomato Pasta

MAKES 4 SERVINGS

2 tablespoons **olive oil**

3 boneless, skinless **chicken breast** halves, cut into bite-size pieces

3 to 4 cups **broccoli**, chopped

½ of an 8-ounce jar **sun-dried tomatoes**

Fresh **garlic**

1-pound package fresh **mushrooms**, sliced

4 tablespoons **sun-dried tomato pesto**

½ cup **half & half**

2 tablespoons **butter**

1 to 2 tablespoons of the oil from **sun-dried tomatoes**

Salt and **pepper** to taste

8 ounces whole grain **angel hair pasta**

Parmesan or **Asiago cheese**, shredded

1 Sauté chicken breast pieces in olive oil in a large skillet over medium heat.

2 Remove the chicken from the pan with a slotted spoon and cover to keep warm.

3 Sauté broccoli, garlic and mushrooms in the same skillet.

4 Return 4 tablespoons chicken to the skillet and add sun-dried tomatoes.

5 Mix together pesto, half & half, butter, oil from sun-dried tomatoes, salt and pepper.

6 Pour the pesto mixture and the remaining chicken into skillet and simmer over low heat.

7 Cook pasta according to directions and drain.

8 To serve, place pasta on a serving dish and top with chicken and vegetable sauce.

9 Sprinkle cheese over dish before serving.

Roast Turkey *with* Wild Rice *and* Pecan Stuffing

MAKES 12-14 SERVINGS

14- to 16-pound **turkey**
3 tablespoons **butter**
1 tablespoon **honey**
½ teaspoon **salt**
½ teaspoon fresh ground **pepper**
2 cups **chicken broth**
½ cup **water**

Wild Rice and Pecan Stuffing
7 cups **chicken stock** or **broth**
1½ cups **wild rice**
1½ cups **long-grain rice**
½ cup **butter**
2 medium **onions**, chopped
1½ cups **celery**, chopped
1 large can sliced **mushrooms**
2 large cloves **garlic**, minced
1 teaspoon **poultry seasoning**
¼ cup **white wine**
2 **eggs**, beaten

1 Preheat oven to 425°F.

2 Rinse bird and pat dry.

3 Spoon stuffing into the neck and cavities.

4 Skewer openings and place turkey on a rack in a large roasting pan.

5 Melt the butter and add honey, salt and pepper.

6 Brush mixture over the turkey.

7 Pour broth and water into the pan.

8 Roast for 45 minutes.

9 Reduce the heat to 350°F.

10 Cover with aluminum foil and continue cooking until a meat thermometer registers 175°F (about 2 hours and 20 minutes). Add more water if needed.

Wild Rice and Pecan Stuffing

1 Bring stock to a boil.

2 Add the rice, reduce heat, cover and simmer 30 minutes, until the rice is tender and the stock is absorbed.

3 Transfer to a large mixing bowl.

4 Melt ½ cup butter in a large skillet over medium heat.

1 cup **pecans**, chopped
¼ cup **parsley**, chopped
Salt and **pepper** to taste

Gravy
4 cups of **broth** and **stock**
  mixed together
¼ cup **butter**
6 tablespoons **flour**
Salt and **pepper** to taste

5 Add onions and celery and sauté for 10 minutes.

6 Add mushrooms, garlic and seasoning, cooking until tender, about 8 to 10 minutes.

7 Add wine and bring to a boil.

8 Pour mixture over rice.

9 Stir in eggs, remaining stock, pecans and parsley.

10 Season to taste with salt and pepper.

Gravy

1 Pour pan juices into a measuring cup and remove the grease.

2 Add enough broth to make 4½ cups.

3 Melt butter in a large saucepan over low heat.

4 Add flour and stir until golden brown, approximately 5 minutes.

5 Gradually whisk in stock and bring to a boil.

6 Reduce heat and simmer until thickened.

7 Season to taste with salt and pepper.

Chicken *and* Stuffing Casserole

MAKES 6 SERVINGS

3 cups **chicken** or **turkey**, cooked

1 stick **butter**, melted

2½ cups **cornbread stuffing mix**

10.75-ounce can **cream of mushroom soup**

10.75-ounce can **cream of chicken soup**

2 cups **chicken broth**

1 Chop chicken or turkey into small pieces.

2 Mix the butter with the stuffing in a large bowl.

3 Blend together the soups and the broth in a separate mixing bowl.

4 Place the stuffing mixture in the bottom of a 2-quart casserole dish, buttered or coated with cooking spray.

5 Layer the casserole dish with half of the chicken, then half of the soup mixture. Repeat layers.

6 Bake at 350°F for 30 minutes.

Pasta Carbonara

MAKES 6 SERVINGS

6 ounces **bacon**, sliced

2 cloves **garlic**, minced

¾ pound **spaghetti**, cooked and drained

¼ cup **Parmesan cheese**, grated

2 tablespoons **parsley**, chopped

¼ teaspoon **black pepper**

1 cup **whipping cream**

4 **egg yolks**

1 Brown the bacon in a large skillet until crispy.

2 Remove the bacon and place on a paper towel to drain.

3 Add the garlic to the pan and cook in the bacon fat for only 20 seconds.

4 Reduce the heat to low and add the cooked spaghetti.

5 Toss the spaghetti in the skillet; then add the Parmesan cheese, parsley and pepper.

6 Combine the cream and egg yolks in a mixing bowl and stir well.

7 Pour mixture into the skillet with the spaghetti and cook until the mixture thickens—about 3 to 4 minutes.

8 Adjust seasonings to taste and serve.

Autumn Chicken *with* Baked Rice Pilaf

MAKES 8 SERVINGS

8 boneless **chicken breasts**

1 tablespoon **garlic**, minced

1 tablespoon dried **oregano**

Salt and **pepper** to taste

1 cup **red wine vinegar**

½ cup **olive oil**

2 cups **prunes**, pitted

2 cups **dried apricots**

2 cups **green olives**

½ cup **capers**, with juice

8 **bay leaves**

1 cup **brown sugar**

1 cup **dry white wine**

4 teaspoons **parsley**, chopped

Baked Rice Pilaf

½ cup **onion**, finely diced

4 tablespoons **unsalted butter**

1 cup **long-grain rice**

2 cups **chicken stock**

4 **bay leaves**

½ cup fresh **parsley**, chopped

1 Cut chicken into bite-size pieces.

2 Combine garlic, oregano, seasonings, vinegar, oil, fruits, olives, capers and bay leaves in a plastic container.

3 Add chicken and marinate in refrigerator overnight.

4 Transfer to a 9x13-inch casserole dish.

5 Sprinkle with brown sugar and pour wine over the chicken.

6 Cover with parchment paper and aluminum foil and bake for 1½ hours at 350°F.

7 Serve with Baked Rice Pilaf.

Baked Rice Pilaf

1 Sauté onion in butter over medium heat until transparent, about 5 minutes.

2 Add rice and stir to coat well with butter.

3 Add chicken stock and bay leaves.

4 Transfer rice to a 2-quart, oven-proof casserole dish, cover with aluminum foil and bake at 375°F on the lowest rack in the oven for 24-28 minutes or until all of the stock has been absorbed.

5 Remove from oven, remove the bay leaves and stir in the fresh parsley.

Taco Lasagna

MAKES 6 SERVINGS

1½ pounds **ground beef**

1 cup **onion**, chopped

1½ cups **green pepper**, chopped

4.5-ounce can **green chili peppers**

2.5-ounce package **taco seasoning**

2 cups **taco sauce**

3 cups **Colby-Jack cheese**

10 **flour tortillas**

1 Brown the ground beef.

2 Add the onion, pepper, chilies and taco seasoning.

3 Spread ½ cup of the taco sauce in the bottom of a coated 9x13-inch casserole dish.

4 Layer with 5 of the tortillas, folded in half to fit across the dish.

5 Layer with half of the meat mixture, ¾ cup of the taco sauce and 1½ cups of the cheese; repeat.

6 Bake at 375°F for 15 to 20 minutes or until the cheese is melted.

Baked Kentucky Trout *with* Prosciutto

MAKES 4 SERVINGS

4 fresh Kentucky **trout**, boned

4 sprigs **rosemary**

¼ pound **prosciutto** or **country ham**, cut in strips

8 teaspoons **butter**

Salt

Pepper

Paprika

Dry white wine

1 Top each fish with a sprig of rosemary, a strip of ham or prosciutto and 1 teaspoon butter.

2 Roll up the fish and secure with a wooden toothpick.

3 Place the fish in a buttered baking dish and dot each fish with another teaspoon of butter.

4 Dust with salt, pepper and paprika.

5 Bake at 350°F for 10 minutes per inch of thickness of the fish (measured in thickest part).

6 Baste with pan juices periodically.

7 Remove from the oven and top the fish with another piece of ham or prosciutto and a drizzle of wine.

8 Broil for about a minute to make the ham crisp.

Dennis' Chicken

MAKES 8 SERVINGS

8 boneless, skinless
  chicken breasts
Swiss cheese
Bacon
White wine
Teriyaki sauce (preferably
  Kikkoman)
Sliced **mushrooms**
Parmesan cheese

1 Flatten breasts with a meat tenderizer or edge of a plate.

2 Place chicken on top of bacon; place a strip of cheese on top of chicken.

3 Roll up breast, with the bacon strip on the outside.

4 Secure with a toothpick and place seam side down in a baking dish.

5 Mix equal amounts of teriyaki sauce and white wine and pour over chicken.

6 Top with mushrooms and Parmesan cheese to taste.

7 Bake at 350°F for 30 to 45 minutes.

Em's Beer-Battered Pork Chops *with* 1-Hour Sauerkraut

MAKES 4 SERVINGS

Pork Chops

4 thick **pork loin chops**, butterflied, if desired
1 teaspoon **garlic powder**
½ teaspoon **salt**
½ teaspoon **pepper**
½ teaspoon **Hungarian paprika**
12-ounce can of your favorite **beer**
10-.75-ounce can **cream of mushroom soup**
1 tablespoon **stone-ground mustard**
Splash **Worcestershire sauce**
¼ cup **corn flake** crumbs or regular **bread crumbs**

1 Season chops on both sides with garlic powder, salt, pepper and paprika.

2 Brown chops in olive oil, cooking in frying pan on both sides to sear in flavor.

3 Combine beer, cream of mushroom soup, Worcestershire sauce and mustard in a medium bowl.

4 Remove chops from frying pan and transfer to oven-safe dish. Pour beer mixture over chops and bake at 350°F for 1 hour.

5 Take chops out and turn oven to broiler setting.

6 Sprinkle top of chops with corn flake crumbs and broil 1-2 minutes until flakes are golden brown.

Submitted by Emily Braun of Cincinnati, Ohio, this recipe was the winner of the Main Course category in Kentucky Monthly's 2010 Recipe Contest.

1-Hour Sauerkraut

1 medium head
  cabbage, green or
  purple, roughly
  shredded
1 large **apple**, peeled and
  roughly chopped or
  shredded
1¼ cup **cider vinegar**
¼ cup **white vinegar**
¼ cup **water**
Splash **sherry**
1 tablespoon **kosher salt**
½ teaspoon **fennel seed**
½ teaspoon **celery salt**
Dash **Hungarian paprika**
2 tablespoons **bacon**,
  cooked, chopped and
  well-drained

1-Hour Sauerkraut

1 Combine all ingredients except bacon in a large pot
and bring to a boil.

2 Reduce heat, cover and simmer 40 minutes.

3 Add bacon and simmer an additional 10 minutes.

Bourbon-Braised Brussels Sprouts *with* Bacon

MAKES 8 SERVINGS

½ pound hickory-smoked **bacon**, chopped

2½ pounds fresh **Brussels sprouts**

¼ cup **shallots**, sliced

1 cup Kentucky **bourbon**

¼ cup **apple juice**

2 tablespoons **honey**

Kosher salt

Freshly ground **black pepper**

1 In a heavy skillet, cook bacon over medium heat until it browns.

2 Clean sprouts and cut off tough ends.

3 Cut a criss-cross on the bottom of each (to help the sprouts cook more quickly).

4 Drain away most of the bacon fat from the pan and add sprouts and shallots to the cooked bacon. Stir often.

5 Mix together bourbon, apple juice and honey; once shallots begin to caramelize, add bourbon mixture.

6 Turn up heat.

7 When the liquid starts to boil, reduce heat and simmer, uncovered, for 30 minutes, or until braising liquid has reduced by half and sprouts have become tender.

8 Add salt and black pepper to taste.

Carson House Corn Pudding

MAKES 8 SERVINGS

12 ounces frozen **corn**

15-ounce can **creamed corn**

8 tablespoons all-purpose **flour**

1 teaspoon **kosher salt**

2 heaping teaspoons **sugar**

4 tablespoons **butter**, melted

4 large **eggs**, beaten

2 cups whole **milk**

1 cup **half & half**

½ cup **Parmesan cheese**, grated

1 Stir together the frozen corn, creamed corn, flour, salt, sugar and butter in a large mixing bowl.

2 Whisk the eggs with the milk and half & half; stir into the corn mixture.

3 Pour the mixture into a 2-quart, coated baking dish and bake at 450°F for about 45 minutes.

4 Stir with a long-pronged fork several times during baking.

5 During the last 10 minutes of baking, sprinkle grated Parmesan cheese on top.

Owned by Bob and Norma Laufer, the Carson House is in Old Louisville.

Stuffed Acorn Squash

MAKES 8 SERVINGS

3 slices **bacon**

4 baked **acorn squash**

3 tablespoons **onion**, chopped

5 tablespoons **butter**

½ cup **soft bread crumbs**

¼ cup **water**

1 **egg**

½ teaspoon **salt**

⅛ teaspoon **pepper**

½ cup **dry bread crumbs**

1 teaspoon **sugar**

1 Fry bacon until crisp; crumble and set aside.

2 Remove squash from shells and mash.

3 Brown onion in two tablespoons butter.

4 Soak soft bread crumbs in water; mash and add to onion.

5 Add squash and cook about 15 minutes, stirring occasionally.

6 Stir in egg.

7 Add salt and pepper, sugar and half of bacon.

8 Place mixture in squash shells.

9 Mix remainder of bacon with dry bread crumbs.

10 Sprinkle over squash and dot with the remaining butter.

11 Bake at 375°F for about 20 minutes or until browned.

Scalloped Oysters

MAKES 12 SERVINGS

4 12-ounce containers
fresh oysters
½ pound butter **crackers**,
crumbled
½ pound plain **soda
crackers**, crumbled
½ teaspoon fresh ground
pepper
1 stick **butter**
1 to 1½ cups **heavy cream**

1 Drain oysters, reserving the liquid.

2 Mix cracker crumbs together.

3 Place a third of the crumbs in the bottom of a shallow, buttered 9x13-inch casserole dish.

4 Add a layer of half the oysters, sprinkle with pepper and dot with half of the butter.

5 Make a second layer and top with crumbs; dot with remaining butter.

6 Combine oyster liquid and cream.

7 Pour the oyster cream evenly over the casserole.

8 Bake at 400°F for 25 to 30 minutes.

Red Skin Garlic Mashed Potatoes

MAKES 4-6 SERVINGS

10 to 12 **red potatoes**, uniformly sized

2 to 3 cloves **garlic**, thinly sliced

Salt and **pepper** to taste

¾ stick **butter**

½ to ¾ cup **sour cream**

1 Scrub but do not peel potatoes; remove any blemishes.

2 Boil whole potatoes and garlic until thoroughly cooked; drain.

3 Lightly mash potatoes and garlic, leaving some lumps.

4 Mix in seasonings, butter and sour cream.

Sweet Potatoes *in* Orange Rinds

MAKES 12 SERVINGS

6 medium-size **oranges**

4 medium **sweet potatoes**

4 tablespoons **orange juice concentrate**, undiluted

3 tablespoons **butter**, melted

½ teaspoon **salt**

Pinch of **pepper**

1 teaspoon **orange flavoring**, *optional*

¼ cup **granulated sugar**

¼ cup **brown sugar**

1 teaspoon **cinnamon**

3 tablespoons **butter**, melted

3 tablespoons **walnuts** or **pecans**, chopped

Miniature marshmallows, *optional*

1 Cut oranges in half; squeeze juice and use a serrated fruit spoon to remove the fruit and membrane from the orange rind.

2 Boil sweet potatoes until tender and drain.

3 Cool slightly, peel and mash with the orange juice concentrate, butter, salt, pepper, flavoring and granulated sugar. Mix well.

4 Fill the orange shells with sweet potato mixture.

5 Mix together brown sugar, cinnamon, butter and nuts and top potatoes with the mixture.

6 Place sweet potato-filled oranges on a baking sheet and bake at 350°F for 15 to 20 minutes.

7 Miniature marshmallows may be added, if desired.

TIP: *Thin-skinned oranges work best for this recipe.*

Creamed Spinach

MAKES 4 SERVINGS

½ cup **whipping cream**

2 tablespoons **unsalted butter**

½ teaspoon **salt**

Freshly ground **pepper** to taste

¼ teaspoon **nutmeg**

1 pound fresh **spinach**, stems removed

1 Heat the cream and butter together in a saucepan.

2 Add the salt, pepper and nutmeg; set aside.

3 Steam the spinach in a vegetable steamer or a covered pot with only a little water until just wilted, about 3 or 4 minutes; remove from heat.

4 Pour the spinach into a colander and drain from it as much water as possible by pressing it with the back of a wooden spoon.

5 Put the spinach into a food processor and pulse a few times to chop.

6 Add the hot cream mixture to the spinach and continue to pulse a few more times.

7 Pour the mixture into a serving bowl, reheat in the microwave briefly and serve topped with freshly ground nutmeg.

Broccoli *and* Cheese Casserole

MAKES 6 SERVINGS

1 pound fresh **broccoli**, cut into small pieces

10.75-ounce can **cream of mushroom soup**

2 large **eggs**, lightly beaten

1 cup **mayonnaise**

1½ cups **cheddar cheese**, shredded

1 stick **butter**

Pepper

1 sleeve **butter crackers**, crushed

1 Coat a 9x13-inch baking dish with cooking spray.

2 Steam the broccoli until crisp-tender—about 7 minutes.

3 Transfer the broccoli to a bowl of ice water to cool.

4 Mix the soup, eggs, mayonnaise, cheese, butter and pepper in a saucepan and cook over medium-low heat, stirring constantly until cheese has melted and ingredients have combined.

5 Drain broccoli and spread evenly in the baking dish.

6 Pour cheese mixture on top. Sprinkle with cracker crumbs.

7 Bake at 350°F for 30 minutes.

Red Potato Casserole

MAKES 6-8 SERVINGS

10 medium **red potatoes**
⅓ cup **milk**
½ **green pepper**, diced
½ **red pepper**, diced
1 **onion**, chopped
1 tablespoon fresh
    parsley, chopped
½ cup sharp **cheddar
    cheese**, grated
¼ cup **butter**, melted
Salt and **pepper** to taste

1 Boil potatoes in skins for 25 minutes or until just tender.

2 Drain, cool and dice into bite-size pieces.

3 Place potatoes in a large greased baking dish; potatoes should be in a single layer.

4 Pour milk over the potatoes.

5 Combine peppers, onion, parsley and cheese; mix and spread on top of potatoes.

6 Pour melted butter over all and season.

7 Bake, uncovered, at 400°F for 30 minutes or until golden brown.

Broccoli *and* Brown Rice Casserole

MAKES 4 SERVINGS

10 ounces frozen **broccoli**, chopped

4 tablespoons **butter**

1 cup **cheddar cheese**, shredded

½ cup uncooked, instant **brown rice**

½ cup **water**

½ teaspoon **salt**

¼ teaspoon **pepper**

12 crushed **butter crackers**

2 tablespoons **butter**, melted

1 Cook the broccoli according to directions and drain well.

2 Mix the broccoli, butter, cheese, rice, water, salt and pepper.

3 Pour the mixture into a greased 1½-quart baking dish and top with crushed crackers.

4 Drizzle melted butter over crackers.

5 Bake at 350°F for 30 minutes or until top is brown and the dish bubbles.

See page 233 for photo.

Pumpkin Cupcakes *with* Orange Cream Cheese Icing

MAKES 12 CUPCAKES

½ cup **butter**
1 cup **sugar**
2 large **eggs**
1 cup canned **pumpkin**
1 teaspoon **vanilla**
1½ cups all-purpose **flour**
2 teaspoons **baking powder**
½ teaspoon **cinnamon**
¼ teaspoon **nutmeg**
¼ teaspoon ground **cloves**
¼ teaspoon **salt**
¼ cup **milk**

Orange Cream Cheese Icing
6 ounces **cream cheese**
6 tablespoons **butter**
1½ to 2 cups **powdered sugar**
1 tablespoon **orange peel**, finely minced
¼ to ½ teaspoon **orange extract**
Candy corn, *optional*

1 Combine butter and sugar in a mixing bowl with an electric beater.

2 Add eggs, beating well after each addition.

3 Add pumpkin and vanilla and mix well.

4 In a separate bowl combine flour, baking powder, cinnamon, nutmeg, cloves and salt.

5 Stir half the flour mixture into pumpkin mixture.

6 Stir in milk just until blended.

7 Add remaining flour mixture and stir just until incorporated.

8 Spoon batter into 12 lined muffin cups, filling each cup about three-quarters full.

9 Bake at 350°F until tops spring back when lightly pressed—about 20 minutes.

10 Let cool in pans for 5 minutes; remove cupcakes from pans and cool at least 30 minutes.

Orange Cream Cheese Icing
1 Beat the cream cheese and butter, both at room temperature, until well blended.

2 Add the powdered sugar, orange peel and extract and beat until smooth.

3 Spread or pipe icing onto cooled cakes. Decorate with candy corn, if desired.

David Dominé's Apple Stack Cakes *with* Bourbon Whipped Cream

MAKES 12 SERVINGS

2 cups granulated **sugar**

1 cup **butter**, softened

2 large **eggs**

6 cups all-purpose **flour**

3 teaspoons **baking powder**

1 teaspoon **baking soda**

½ teaspoon **salt**

1 cup **buttermilk**

1 tablespoon **vanilla extract**

Apple Filling

16 ounces **dried apples**

1 cup light **brown sugar**

1 teaspoon ground **cinnamon**

¼ teaspoon ground **cloves**

¼ teaspoon ground **allspice**

1 Preheat oven to 400°F.

2 Cream the sugar and butter in a large bowl.

3 Add eggs, one at a time, beating well after each addition.

4 Sift together dry ingredients and add to butter mixture, alternating with buttermilk and vanilla extract. Mix well.

5 Divide dough into eight equal parts.

6 To form the cake layers, pat each of the eight pieces of dough into its own well-greased 9-inch pan. It is important that the rounds be uniform in size.

7 Bake layers on a cookie sheet for 10 to 15 minutes until browned; cool on wire racks.

8 Allow the layers to cool.

9 Once the layers have cooled, spread each with apple filling and layer. Top with bourbon whipped cream.

Apple Filling

1 Cook apples with the sugar and spices in enough water to cover until soft.

2 Once cooked, cool and puree before spreading between layers.

Bourbon Whipped Cream
2 cups **heavy cream**
½ cup **powdered sugar**
2 tablespoons Kentucky
bourbon

Bourbon Whipped Cream

1 Whip heavy cream with powdered sugar and bourbon.

David Dominé, aka The Bluegrass Peasant, is the dining correspondent for Kentucky Monthly. This recipe is from Dominé's cookbook Adventures in New Kentucky Cooking.

Spiced Apple Cookies *with* Vanilla Glaze

MAKES 3 DOZEN

½ cup **shortening**

1⅓ cups packed **brown sugar**

1 **egg**

¼ cup **milk**

2 cups all-purpose **flour**

1 teaspoon **baking soda**

1 teaspoon **nutmeg**

1 teaspoon **cinnamon**

½ teaspoon **cloves**

1 cup **walnuts,** chopped

1 cup **apple**, peeled and finely diced

1 cup **raisins**

Vanilla Glaze

1½ cups **powdered sugar**

1 tablespoon **butter,** melted

½ teaspoon **vanilla extract**

⅛ teaspoon **salt**

2 teaspoons **milk**

1 Cream the shortening and brown sugar in a large mixing bowl.

2 Beat in egg and milk.

3 Combine flour, baking soda, nutmeg, cinnamon and cloves; gradually add to the creamed mixture.

4 Stir in walnuts, apple and raisins.

5 Drop by rounded tablespoonfuls 2 inches apart onto an uncoated baking sheet. Bake at 400°F for 8 to 10 minutes or until the edges begin to brown. Remove to wire racks.

Vanilla Glaze

1 Combine the powdered sugar, butter, vanilla extract, salt and enough milk to achieve drizzling consistency.

2 Drizzle over warm cookies.

The J.P. Rehm House Chocolate Chess Pie

MAKES 8 SERVINGS

1½ cups granulated **sugar**

3½ tablespoons **cocoa powder**

2 **eggs**, beaten

⅔ cup **evaporated milk**

¼ cup **butter**, melted

1¼ teaspoons **vanilla extract**

¼ teaspoon **salt**

9-inch **pie crust**

Vanilla or **butter pecan ice cream**

1 Combine the sugar, cocoa, eggs, evaporated milk, butter, vanilla extract and salt in a mixing bowl; stir until smooth.

2 Pour the mixture into the uncooked pie shell and bake at 325°F for 50 minutes, or until the entire surface puffs up.

3 Cover with foil if outer crust becomes too brown.

4 Remove from the oven and cool on a wire rack.

5 Cut into wedges and top each piece with a scoop of vanilla or butter pecan ice cream.

This recipe comes to us from Mike and Candace Milligan, owners of The J.P. Rehm House in Old Louisville.

Pecan Delights

MAKES 10 SERVINGS

2 cups self-rising **flour**
⅔ cup **brown sugar**
¾ cup **butter**, softened
½ cup **brown sugar**
½ cup Kentucky **honey**
⅔ cup **butter**
3 tablespoons **whipping cream**
1 teaspoon **vanilla extract**
2 **eggs**, beaten
2 cups **pecans**, chopped

1 Cut together the flour, ⅔ cup brown sugar and ¾ cup butter using a pastry blender.

2 Pour mixture into two lightly greased, 9-inch pie plates or one lightly greased 9x13-inch baking dish.

3 Pat mixture onto dish bottom and up the sides. Top with pecans.

4 Place ½ cup brown sugar, honey and ⅔ cup butter in a saucepan and bring to a boil, stirring constantly.

5 Add the cream and vanilla and continue stirring.

6 Gradually add the hot mixture into the beaten eggs a small amount at a time, stirring constantly until all is added.

7 When entire mixture is incorporated into the egg mixture, pour contents into the pie crusts.

8 Bake at 350°F for 25 to 30 minutes, or until top is golden brown.

9 Cool before cutting into squares or slivers of pie.

Carrot Bars *with* Cream Cheese Frosting

MAKES 24 SQUARES

4 **eggs**
2 cups **sugar**
1 cup **vegetable oil**
3 cups **carrots**, grated
1 teaspoon **vanilla**
2 cups self-rising **flour**
2 teaspoons **baking soda**
2 teaspoons **cinnamon**
1 teaspoon **allspice**
¼ teaspoon **cloves**
½ cup **nuts**, chopped

Cream Cheese Frosting
4 tablespoons **butter**, softened
3-ounce package **cream cheese**, softened
2 cups **powdered sugar**
2 teaspoons **vanilla**

1 Beat the eggs, sugar and oil in a large mixing bowl.

2 Add the carrots and vanilla and mix well.

3 Combine the dry ingredients and add to the carrot mixture.

4 Fold in the nuts.

5 Pour into a coated 15x10x2-inch baking pan.

6 Bake at 350°F for 30 minutes.

7 Allow the cake to cool completely.

8 Spread the cream cheese frosting over the cooled cake.

9 Cut into bars.

Cream Cheese Frosting

1 Combine the butter and cream cheese in a mixing bowl and beat well.

2 Add powdered sugar and vanilla and blend well.

Apple Bourbon Upside-Down Cake

MAKES 6 SERVINGS

¾ cup **unsalted butter**, softened, plus extra for greasing the pan

⅓ cup **brown sugar**

½ cup Kentucky **bourbon**

3 large, crisp Granny Smith **apples**, peeled, cored and sliced

1 tablespoon fresh **lemon juice**

½ teaspoon ground **cinnamon**

2 teaspoons **salt**

2 cups all-purpose **flour**

1 teaspoon **baking powder**

¾ cup granulated **sugar**

2 large **eggs**, at room temperature

1 teaspoon pure **vanilla extract**

½ cup **buttermilk**

1 Preheat oven to 350°F.

2 Butter a 9-inch springform pan.

3 In a saucepan, melt 4 tablespoons of butter over medium heat.

4 To the melted butter, add brown sugar and ¼ cup bourbon; stir until bubbly. Remove from heat.

5 Toss apples with lemon juice, cinnamon and a pinch of salt.

6 Pour butter mixture and arrange slices in a spiral pattern in pan.

7 Whisk flour, baking powder and remaining salt in a bowl; set aside.

8 Beat remaining butter in a mixer with a paddle attachment until smooth.

9 Add granulated sugar and beat on medium speed until light and fluffy.

10 Add eggs, one at a time, and beat until incorporated.

11 Add vanilla and reduce speed to low.

12 Add half of the flour mixture, buttermilk and remaining bourbon.

13 Mix until combined and add the rest of flour mixture.

14 Pour mixture over apples.

15 Bake until golden and center springs back, about 35 minutes.

16 Cool on a wire rack for 5 minutes.

17 Flip pan onto a serving plate and let stand, then lift pan.

18 Serve warm.

German Chocolate Cheesecake

MAKES 12 SERVINGS

1 cup **chocolate wafer** crumbs

2 tablespoons **sugar**

3 tablespoons **butter**, melted

24 ounces **cream cheese**, softened

¾ cup **sugar**

¼ cup **cocoa**

2 teaspoons **vanilla extract**

3 large **eggs**

⅓ cup **evaporated milk**

⅓ cup **sugar**

¼ cup **butter**

Pinch of **salt**

1 large **egg**, lightly beaten

½ teaspoon **vanilla extract**

½ cup **pecans**, chopped

½ cup **flaked coconut**

1 Stir together the wafer crumbs, 2 tablespoons sugar and butter; press into the bottom of a 9-inch springform pan.

2 Bake at 325°F for 10 minutes; let cool.

3 Beat the cream cheese, ¾ cup sugar, cocoa and vanilla at medium speed with an electric mixer until blended.

4 Add the eggs, one at a time, beating just until blended after each addition.

5 Pour into the prepared crust and bake for 35 to 45 minutes.

6 Remove from oven and loosen cake from the pan; cool. Chill 8 hours.

7 Stir together the evaporated milk, ⅓ cup sugar, ¼ cup butter, salt and egg in a saucepan.

8 Add the vanilla and cook over medium heat, stirring constantly, for about 7 minutes to thicken.

9 Stir in the pecans and coconut; cool slightly and spread over the cheesecake.

Fresh Apple Cake

MAKES 12 SERVINGS

1 cup **cooking oil**

2 cups **sugar**

3 **eggs**

2 cups self-rising **flour**

3 cups fresh **apples**, chopped

1 teaspoon **vanilla**

1 cup **pecans** or black **walnuts**

½ cup **raisins** (optional)

1 teaspoon **cinnamon**

1 teaspoon **nutmeg**

Cream Cheese and Nut Icing:

1 stick **butter**

3 ounces **cream cheese**

1 pound **confectioners' sugar**

⅓ cup **nuts**, chopped

½ teaspoon **vanilla**

1 Combine oil, sugar and eggs and beat well.

2 Add flour slowly and continue to beat.

3 Pour in remaining ingredients and stir well.

4 Pour mixture into greased, 9x12x2-inch cake pan.

5 Bake at 350°F for 40 to 45 minutes.

6 Allow the cake to cool completely.

7 Spread cream cheese icing on the cooled cake and refrigerate.

Cream Cheese and Nut Icing

1 Cream together butter, cream cheese and confectioners' sugar until spreading consistency is reached.

2 Add nuts and vanilla.

Pear Frangipani Tart

MAKES 8 SERVINGS

11-inch unbaked **pie shell**, chilled

4 ounces **unsalted butter**

½ cup granulated **sugar**

1 **egg**

1 cup blanched **almonds**, finely ground

1 tablespoon all-purpose **flour**

3 tablespoons **dark rum**

1 teaspoon **almond extract**

4 **pears**

1 cup **sugar**

1 cup **apple** or **plum jelly**, warmed

1 Preheat oven to 425°F. Place the pie shell in a tart pan with a removable bottom.

2 Cream together the butter and sugar in a mixing bowl until light and fluffy. Add egg, almonds, flour, rum and almond extract and beat until smooth.

3 Spread the thick mixture evenly into the chilled tart shell and refrigerate while preparing the pears.

4 Peel pears and cut in half. Place pears, cut side down, in large pot with 4 cups of water and 1 cup of sugar to make a poaching liquid. Simmer pears 20 minutes, and then plunge into ice water.

5 When cooled, remove core and stem from pears. Place each half, cut side down, on a cutting board and cut crosswise into thin slices.

6 Arrange slices, placing the top, or thinnest part, toward the middle of the frangipani. Pull slices toward the center of the tart, which will elongate the pears a bit and fill the shell.

7 Bake for 45 minutes or until tart shell is golden brown and frangipani has puffed and browned.

8 Brush the tart with warm jelly.

WINTER

Frost and snow carpet the Kentucky scenery with a silvery glow, while the safety of hearth and home eases the winter chill. The flavors of the coldest season are rich and robust and sometimes sinfully sugared.

Comfort foods such as Southwest Noodle Bake, White Lasagna and Baked Crab Macaroni and Cheese, and the substantial tastes of Beef Tenderloin and Steak with Brandy Cream Sauce offer a reprieve from winter weariness. Add to these a decadent assortment of desserts, and you have such stuff as both dreams and New Year's resolutions are made on.

Relax in the comfort of your Kentucky home as you enjoy the following recipes of winter.

Cheesy Chick Appetizers

MAKES 18 SERVINGS

¾ cup **chicken**, roasted and chopped

1 tablespoon **mayonnaise**

½ cup **green olives**, chopped

¼ cup **garden vegetable cream cheese**, softened

2 tablespoons **walnuts**, chopped

9 sheets frozen **phyllo dough**, thawed

Cooking spray

Butter, melted

1 Mix together the chicken, mayonnaise, olives, cream cheese and walnuts.

2 Unwrap phyllo dough, unroll and cover with a damp kitchen towel.

3 Place 1 sheet of dough on a clean surface and spray with cooking spray.

4 Top with 2 more sprayed sheets.

5 Gently cut the dough with scissors to make 3 long strips. Then cut the strips in half.

6 Place a tablespoon of chicken and cheese mixture at the end of one strip and roll it up like a flag, making a triangle. Press the ends to seal.

7 Repeat the process with the other phyllo, using 3 sprayed sheets each time until all of the sheets and mixture are used.

8 Place triangles on an ungreased baking sheet; brush with melted butter.

9 Bake at 375°F about 10 minutes or until appetizers are lightly browned.

Gruyère-Chive Mini Popovers

MAKES 24 PIECES

Canola oil, for greasing pans
1 cup **flour**
½ teaspoon **salt**
¼ teaspoon **freshly ground pepper**
1 tablespoon **fresh chives**, finely snipped
1¼ cups **milk**, at room temperature
2 **eggs**, at room temperature
1 tablespoon **unsalted butter**, melted
3 ounces **Gruyère cheese**, coarsely grated

1 Preheat the oven to 450°F.

2 Generously grease 1 large or 2 small mini muffin pans.

3 Whisk the flour, salt, pepper and chives in a large bowl.

4 Whisk the milk, eggs and butter in a large measuring pitcher.

5 Pour the wet ingredients over the dry ingredients and whisk together until just combined. Don't worry if some lumps remain.

6 Fill the prepared muffin cups to within about ¼ inch from the rims.

7 Place 1 scant teaspoon grated cheese in the center of each filled cup.

8 Bake, without opening the oven door, for 10 minutes. Reduce the oven temperature to 350°F and bake an additional 8 to 10 minutes or until the popovers are brown, crusty and fully puffed.

9 Transfer the popovers to a platter and serve warm.

Italian Sausage *and* Mozzarella Pinwheels

MAKES 12 SERVINGS

1 tablespoon **flour**
11-ounce packaged roll of **pizza crust**
½ cup **sun-dried tomato pesto**
2 **sweet Italian sausages**
Salt and **pepper** to taste
2 slices **ham**
2 cups **mozzarella cheese**
1 **egg**
1 tablespoon **milk**
¼ cup **Parmesan cheese**

1 Flour the countertop or bread board and roll out pizza crust.

2 Spread tomato pesto sauce on crust to within 1 inch of sides all around.

3 Remove casings from sausages and cook meat over medium-high heat until crumbled and done.

4 Drain sausage and spread over pesto mixture.

5 Dust with salt and pepper to taste.

6 Slice ham and sprinkle over the sausage.

7 Grate fresh mozzarella cheese and spread over sausage and ham mixture.

8 Carefully roll dough to create a long roll, pressing down the top and bottom ends of roll when finished.

9 Beat egg with milk and brush over the dough roll.

10 Sprinkle with Parmesan cheese.

11 Slide roll onto a baking sheet and bake at 400°F for 15 minutes or until nicely browned.

12 Slice the roll at an angle and place on serving tray.

Crostini *with* Steak *and* Horseradish

MAKES 28 PIECES

1½ pounds **flank steak**
3 tablespoons **olive oil**
Salt and **freshly ground pepper** to taste
2 tablespoons **prepared horseradish**
3 tablespoons **sour cream**
1 French **baguette**, cut into ½-inch-thick slices

1 Preheat the oven to 350°F.

2 Brush both sides of the steak with 1 tablespoon of the olive oil; season generously with the salt and pepper.

3 Place the steak on a rack in a roasting pan and let stand at room temperature.

4 Whisk the horseradish and sour cream in a small bowl.

5 Arrange the baguette slices on a baking sheet and brush lightly with the remaining olive oil.

6 Season with salt and pepper and bake about 10 to 15 minutes or until golden.

7 Broil the steak until firm but still quite pink in the center—about 6 minutes per side. Let rest for 5 minutes.

8 Cut the steak with the grain into slices about 2 inches thick, and then cut thin slices crosswise across the grain.

9 Arrange 1 or 2 slices on each crostini and top with a dollop of the horseradish cream.

10 Transfer to a platter and serve at room temperature.

Hot Onion Soufflé Appetizer

3 to 4 cups **onions**, chopped

24 ounces **cream cheese**, softened

2 cups **Parmesan cheese**, grated

½ cup **mayonnaise**

1 Stir together all of the ingredients and place into a 2-quart, buttered casserole.

2 Bake at 425°F about 15 minutes, until golden brown.

3 Serve with assorted crackers or corn chips.

Walnut *and* Rosemary Bread Loaves

MAKES 2 ROUND LOAVES

2 cups **low-fat milk**,
warmed to 100°F-110°F

¼ cup **water**, warmed to
100°F-110°F

3 tablespoons **sugar**

2 tablespoons **butter**,
melted

3 teaspoons **salt**

2 packages **dry yeast**

5½ cups all-purpose **flour**,
divided

1 cup **walnuts**, chopped

3 tablespoons fresh
rosemary, coarsely
chopped

2 large **eggs**, beaten

1 tablespoon **low-fat milk**

Cooking spray

1 Combine the milk, water, sugar, butter and salt in a large mixing bowl and whisk in the yeast. Let stand for 5 minutes.

2 Lightly spoon in 2 cups flour to the yeast mixture and stir well.

3 Cover and let rise in a warm place for 15 minutes.

4 Add 2½ more cups flour, walnuts, rosemary and 1 egg, stirring well.

5 Turn dough out onto a lightly floured surface and knead until smooth, about 10 minutes. Add enough of the remaining flour, ¼ cup at a time, to prevent dough from sticking to your hands.

6 Place dough in a large bowl coated with cooking spray, turning to coat top.

7 Cover and let rise in a warm place for 1 hour or until doubled in size.

8 Punch down dough, turn out onto a lightly floured surface and divide dough in half.

9 Shape each portion into a round and place loaves on a baking sheet coated with cooking spray.

10 Cover and let rise 30 minutes or until doubled in size.

11 Combine 1 tablespoon milk and the remaining egg, whisking until blended, and brush the mixture over the loaves.

12 Make 3 diagonal cuts ¼-inch deep across the tops of the loaves with a sharp knife.

13 Bake at 375°F for 40 minutes. Let stand about 20 minutes before slicing.

Black Bean *and* Rice Salad

MAKES 8 SERVINGS

2 cups **black beans**,
    cooked, or 2 15-ounce
    cans, rinsed and
    drained
2 cups **basmati** or **jasmine**
    rice, cooked
1 cup **olive oil**
¼ cup **lemon juice**
2 cloves **garlic**, minced
2 **green onions**, sliced
Salt and **pepper** to taste
2 tablespoons fresh
    cilantro
Romaine lettuce

1 Combine the cooked beans and rice in a large mixing bowl.

2 Mix together the oil and lemon juice.

3 Add the garlic, green onions, salt and pepper to taste and stir in the cilantro.

4 Pour the dressing over the beans and rice, mix lightly, cover and chill.

5 When ready to serve, tear the desired amount of Romaine lettuce into bite-size pieces and gently mix with the bean, rice and dressing mixture.

Garlic-Stuffed Pork Loin *with* Apple-Bourbon Glaze

MAKES 4 SERVINGS

2 cloves **garlic**
2-pound **boneless pork loin roast**
3 tablespoons **olive oil**
¼ teaspoon **salt**
½ teaspoon **garlic salt**
¼ teaspoon **pepper**
½ teaspoon **rosemary**
½ teaspoon **thyme**

Apple Bourbon Glaze
2 **Gala apples**, peeled, cored and chopped
2 tablespoons **butter**
1 tablespoon **honey**
1 tablespoon Kentucky **bourbon**

1 Peel and thinly slice garlic cloves.

2 Using a sharp knife, cut slits into top of loin, fat side up, and press cloves into slits.

3 Mix the salts, pepper, olive oil, rosemary and thyme in a small mixing bowl.

4 Place pork loin in an 8x8-inch lightly greased baking dish and rub oil mixture all over the loin.

5 Bake uncovered at 350°F for 1 to 1½ hours or until meat thermometer reaches 160°F.

6 Serve Apple Bourbon Glaze over the sliced pork.

Apple Bourbon Glaze

1 Sauté the apples in the butter in a large skillet over medium-high heat.

2 Add the honey and bourbon; continue cooking over low heat until sauce thickens and apples are soft.

Plated with Broccoli and Brown Rice Casserole, for which the recipe can be found on page 199.

White Lasagna

MAKES 6-8 SERVINGS

5 to 6 boneless **chicken breasts**

14.5-ounce can **chicken broth**

3 cups **water**

¼ cup **butter**

1 pound fresh **white mushrooms**, sliced

½ cup **Riesling** or **white cooking wine**

½ teaspoon **tarragon leaves**

¼ cup **butter**

5 tablespoons all-purpose **flour**

½ to 1 teaspoon **salt**

¼ teaspoon **white pepper**

2 cups **half & half**

8 **lasagna noodles**

¼ pound **Swiss cheese**, shredded

½ pound **mozzarella cheese**, shredded

1 Preheat oven to 350°F.

2 Place the chicken in a 4-quart pan. Add broth and water; bring to a boil.

3 Reduce heat, cover and simmer until chicken is tender.

4 Strain broth and reserve.

5 Shred chicken.

6 Melt ¼ cup of butter in a medium pan, add the mushrooms, and then add the wine and tarragon.

7 Cook on medium heat until most of the pan juices have evaporated. Set aside.

8 Melt the remaining ¼ cup butter over medium heat.

9 Blend in the flour, salt and pepper and cook, stirring until bubbly.

10 Remove from heat and gradually stir in half & half and 2½ cups of reserved chicken broth.

11 Return to heat and stir until smooth and thickened.

12 Add the mushroom mixture to the sauce.

13 Spread a thin layer of sauce on the bottom of a 9x13-inch lasagna pan.

14 Arrange the noodles over the sauce, and then place a layer of chicken followed by a layer of sauce and a layer of the cheeses.

15 Repeat layers.

16 Bake until bubbly, approximately 40 minutes.

Submitted by Sherree Loewenberg of Louisville for the Readers' Issue of Kentucky Monthly, *October 2011*

Shrimp *and* White Asparagus Casserole

MAKES 6-8 SERVINGS

2 pounds fresh **white asparagus**
½ cup Kentucky **bourbon**
2 pounds **medium-size shrimp**, whole
¼ cup fresh **parsley**, chopped
2 large **eggs**
1 cup **half & half**
½ teaspoon **kosher salt**
½ teaspoon ground **white pepper**
¼ teaspoon **nutmeg**, freshly grated
1½ cups fresh **bread crumbs**
2 cups **Asiago cheese**, grated
2 tablespoons **olive oil**
2 tablespoons **butter**, melted

1 Preheat oven to 375°F.

2 Clean and trim asparagus. Cut into ½-inch pieces.

3 Transfer asparagus to a saucepan with bourbon and cook, covered, over medium heat for 5 minutes or until the asparagus softens.

4 Drain liquid and reserve while asparagus cools.

5 Clean and de-vein shrimp. Cut into ½-inch pieces.

6 Toss shrimp and asparagus with chopped parsley.

7 Beat eggs and whisk into the cooled bourbon poaching liquid.

8 Add half & half, salt, pepper and nutmeg to the bourbon and egg mixture.

9 Pour mixture over shrimp and asparagus.

10 Fold in ½ cup of bread crumbs and 1 cup of cheese and set aside.

11 Use a pastry brush to grease a large baking dish with olive oil.

12 Coat the bottom and sides of the dish with another ½ cup of bread crumbs.

13 Add shrimp and asparagus mixture and top with remaining cup of cheese.

14 Toss remaining ½ cup of bread crumbs with melted butter sprinkle over cheese.

15 Bake, uncovered, for 40 minutes or until brown and bubbly.

Southwest Noodle Bake

MAKES 6 SERVINGS

1 pound **ground bison**
  (or ground beef)
1 cup **onion**, chopped
Salt, **pepper** and **garlic
  salt** to taste
1½ cups **chunky salsa**
2 cups **light sour cream**
1½ cups **cheddar cheese**,
  shredded
10 ounces **flat egg
  noodles**, uncooked
1 cup **water** or **tomato
  juice**
Cooking spray

1 Coat a frying pan with cooking spray and brown bison and onion; season with salt, pepper and garlic salt.

2 In a bowl, combine the salsa, sour cream and 1 cup of the cheese.

3 Coat a 9x13-inch baking dish with cooking spray, place half of the uncooked noodles in the dish and top with half the meat and onion mixture.

4 Pour half of the salsa/cream mixture over the meat.

5 Place the remaining noodles on top.

6 Add the remaining meat mixture and top with sauce.

7 Sprinkle remaining cheese over the top and drizzle water or tomato juice over all. Be sure to pour liquid around the edges of the pan to properly cook the noodles.

8 Cover with foil and bake at 300°F for 45 minutes; uncover and bake another 15 minutes or until top is brown.

Seafood Creole *with* Brown Rice *with* Carrots

MAKES 6 SERVINGS

1 tablespoon **extra-virgin olive oil**

1 cup **celery**, diced

1 cup **onions**, chopped

3 cloves **garlic**, mashed

½ cup **green pepper**, chopped

14.5-ounce can **diced tomatoes**

½ cup frozen **okra**, unbreaded

1 cup **pasta sauce**

1 teaspoon **Italian seasoning**

2 tablespoons fresh **basil**, minced, or ½ teaspoon dried

2 **tilapia** fillets

16 to 24 **shrimp**, fresh or frozen with the tails off

¼ cup **red wine**

1 Sauté celery and onions in olive oil over medium-high heat.

2 Add garlic and green peppers and cook 2 more minutes.

3 Transfer vegetables to a larger pot and add tomatoes, okra and pasta sauce.

4 Stir in Italian seasoning and basil.

5 Cut fish into 2-inch pieces and add to sauce.

6 Cook over medium-low heat about 10 minutes or until fish is no longer translucent.

7 Add shrimp, red wine and salt and pepper to taste; cook over low heat about 10 minutes.

8 For each serving, pour the fish mixture over the cooked rice.

Brown Rice with Carrots
2 cups instant **brown rice**
2 cups **water**
1 teaspoon **chicken-flavored seasoning**
1 cup **carrots**, shredded
Salt and **pepper** to taste

Brown Rice with Carrots

1 Place rice, water, seasoning and carrots in a covered saucepan and cook on high until mixture begins to boil.

2 Reduce to the lowest heat and cook 10-20 minutes more.

3 Fluff rice and add salt and pepper to taste.

Apricot Glazed Pork Chops *with* Apricot-Apple Stuffing

MAKES 6 SERVINGS

6 **pork chops**, 1-inch thick
¼ cup **flour**
Salt and **pepper** to taste
3 tablespoons **olive oil**

Apricot Glaze
1 cup **apricot preserves**
2 tablespoons **orange juice**
¼ cup Kentucky **bourbon**

Apricot-Apple Stuffing
1 cup **dried apricots**, diced
½ cup boiling **water**
1 tablespoon **Splenda**
4 cups **stale bread**, cubed, any kind
1 large, tart **apple**, peeled and diced
½ teaspoon **thyme**
½ teaspoon **rosemary**
¼ cup **butter**
½ cup **celery**, diced
½ cup **onion**, chopped

1 Coat the pork chops with flour and season with salt and pepper.

2 Brown chops on both sides in a large skillet with the oil.

3 Remove and set aside. Reserve all pan drippings for the stuffing recipe below.

4 Place chops in a single layer on top of the stuffing. Cover and bake at 325°F for 30 minutes.

5 Remove from the oven and pour apricot glaze over the chops.

6 Cover and return to oven. Bake for 1 hour or until chops are thoroughly cooked.

Apricot Glaze

1 Combine ingredients in a small saucepan.

2 Stir over medium heat until well blended.

Apricot-Apple Stuffing

1 Place the apricots in a small bowl and cover with boiling water mixed with sweetener. Set aside.

2 Combine the bread cubes, apple and seasonings in a mixing bowl.

3 Add the butter to the skillet previously used to cook the pork chops.

4 Add celery and onion and sauté until just softened.

5 Drain excess water from the apricots.

6 Gently combine the apricots, sautéed vegetables and bread cube mixture; place in a shallow baking dish that is large enough to hold the pork chops.

Plated with Delicious Carrots with White Grapes, the recipe for which appears on page 248.

Whole Beef Tenderloin

MAKES 6 SERVINGS

3-pound **beef tenderloin**,
trimmed
1 cup **red wine**
¼ cup **Worcestershire
sauce**
½ cup **olive oil**
2 cloves **garlic**, minced
Dash of **sage**

1 Combine wine, Worcestershire sauce, oil, garlic and sage in a mixing bowl and stir well.

2 Place tenderloin in a Ziploc bag, add mixture and marinate overnight in the refrigerator.

3 When ready to cook, remove tenderloin from marinade and place over medium-high gas grill. Cook until internal temperature reaches 125°F for rare to 130°F for medium.

4 Let stand 15 minutes before slicing.

TIP: *The tenderloin also makes great sandwiches for a cocktail party, served thinly sliced on small rolls with horseradish sauce.*

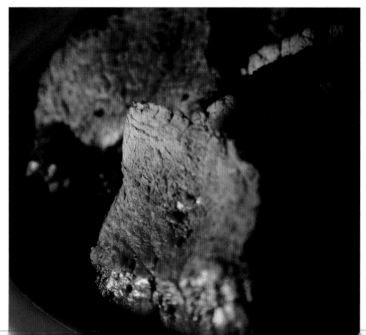

Steak *with* Brandy Cream Sauce

MAKES 2-4 SERVINGS

1 tablespoon **olive oil**
2 8-ounce **beef tenderloin steaks**
Salt and **pepper** to taste

Brandy Cream Sauce
2 **green onions**, thinly sliced
⅓ cup **brandy**
1 cup **whipping cream**

1 Heat the olive oil in a large skillet over medium heat. Sprinkle both sides of the steaks with salt and pepper and add to the hot skillet.

2 Cook for 2 minutes on each side or until brown. Transfer to a 2-quart baking dish. Bake, uncovered, at 400°F for 10 to 13 minutes for medium-rare. Meat should reach an internal temperature of 145°F.

3 Place the steaks on warm serving plates and spoon the brandy cream sauce over the meat.

Brandy Cream Sauce

1 Cook the onions in the same skillet over medium heat, until just tender.

2 Remove skillet from heat, add brandy, and carefully ignite using a long match, because the mixture will flame up. (It is not necessary to ignite the brandy.)

3 Return to heat and simmer, uncovered, for 4 minutes or until most of the liquid has evaporated. When the flame is gone or most of the liquid has evaporated, add the whipping cream. Bring the sauce to a gentle boil for about 8 minutes or until reduced to 1 cup, stirring frequently. Season with salt and pepper.

Luscious Baked Crab Macaroni *and* Cheese

MAKES 10-12 SERVINGS

8 ounces **elbow macaroni**
1 tablespoon **butter**
2 **green onions**, sliced
1 clove **garlic**, minced
1 tablespoon **olive oil**
2 4.5-ounce cans **crabmeat**, drained
2 tablespoons **butter**
2 tablespoons self-rising **flour**
2 cups **half & half**
4 ounces extra sharp white **cheddar cheese**
4 ounces creamy **Havarti cheese**
2 ounces **cream cheese**
½ cup **Parmesan cheese**, grated
Salt and **pepper** to taste
½ cup **panko crumbs**
2 tablespoons **butter**, melted

1 Prepare macaroni noodles according to package directions.

2 Drain, toss with butter and set aside.

3 Sauté onions and garlic in a small skillet over medium high heat with 1 tablespoon olive oil.

4 Add crabmeat and stir for a minute. Set aside.

5 Place butter into a large saucepan over medium heat and add flour.

6 Mix until a smooth roux is formed; add half & half and stir constantly until bubbly.

7 Reduce heat and add cheeses.

8 Stir constantly until cheese melts; pour into a large mixing bowl.

9 Stir in onion, crab mixture, noodles and seasonings, and stir.

10 Pour mixture into a coated, 8x8-inch baking dish.

11 Top with crumbs; drizzle with butter.

12 Bake at 325°F for about 20-25 minutes or until topping is slightly browned and mixture is bubbly.

Not My Mother's Spanish Rice

MAKES 6 SERVINGS

1 cup **rice**, uncooked

2 cups **chicken broth**

6 **tomatoes**, peeled and chopped, or 14.5-ounce can **diced tomatoes**

1 pound **ground beef**

1 tablespoon **olive oil**

19.76 ounces **sweet Italian turkey sausages**

1 **green pepper**, chopped

1 **onion**, chopped

1 tablespoon **Tabasco sauce**

1 Combine rice and broth in a saucepan and bring to a boil.

2 Turn heat down to low and cook until the rice has holes in it, about 25 minutes.

3 Brown beef in a large skillet.

4 Slice and brown sausages in the same skillet.

5 Remove and drain beef and sausages, reserving oil.

6 Add green pepper, onion and hot sauce to the skillet and sauté.

7 Add beef, sausages and tomatoes to skillet.

8 Gently stir in the rice. Mix carefully and warm the mixture on low.

Delicious Carrots *with* White Grapes

6 medium-size **carrots**
1 cup **white grape juice**
1 cup **water**
1 cup **white grapes**, sliced
2 tablespoons **butter**
1 teaspoon **lemon juice**
Salt and **pepper** to taste

1 Slice carrots by hand or in a food processor.

2 Combine carrots, grape juice, lemon juice and water in a medium saucepan and cook on medium heat until carrots are tender.

3 Add grapes, butter and seasonings and reduce heat to low.

4 Simmer until ready to serve.

See photo on page 243.

Frijoles Negros

MAKES 6 SERVINGS

1 pound **black beans**, dry

2½ quarts **water**

1 **green pepper**, cored, seeded and chopped

2 cloves **garlic**, minced

1 medium **onion**, chopped

½ teaspoon **oregano**

½ teaspoon **cumin**

1 **bay leaf**

Garlic salt and **pepper** to taste

½ cup **olive oil**

1 tablespoon **red wine vinegar**

8 to 10 **green olives**

1 Rinse dry beans, place in a large pot and cover with water. Soak overnight.

2 When ready to cook the beans, add into the same water in which you soaked the beans half the green pepper, half the minced garlic, half the chopped onion, oregano, cumin and bay leaf.

3 Bring to a boil and allow to boil a few minutes.

4 Lower the heat and cook about 1 hour or until the beans are tender.

5 Skim the foam off the top of the cooking beans.

6 While the beans are cooking, place oil in a skillet and sauté the remaining green pepper, garlic and onion until the onion is translucent. This mixture is called sofrito.

7 Add garlic salt and pepper to taste.

8 Remove the sofrito from the heat.

9 In a blender, place half the sofrito and approximately one or two ladles of the cooked, tender black beans. Pulse until pureed.

10 Stir the puree and remaining sofrito into the beans.

11 Bring the beans to another boil and simmer until the liquid thickens.

12 Remove bay leaf and add red wine vinegar and the olives to enhance the flavor; cook a few more minutes.

Cream Puffs *with* Mocha Filling

MAKES 12 CREAM PUFFS

1 cup **water**
½ cup **butter**
⅛ teaspoon **salt**
1 cup all-purpose **flour**
4 **eggs**, beaten
¼ cup **powdered sugar**

Mocha Filling
3.4-ounce **chocolate cook
  & serve pudding**
2 cups **milk**
2 tablespoons **instant
  coffee**

1 Preheat oven to 400°F.

2 Combine water, butter and salt in a medium saucepan and cook over medium heat until mixture comes to a full boil.

3 Stir in the flour quickly and mix vigorously with a wooden spoon until it becomes a ball, about a minute.

4 Remove the pan from the heat, add the eggs and beat again by hand until the mixture becomes smooth.

5 Drop dough by ¼ cupfuls about 3 inches apart on an ungreased baking sheet.

6 Bake for 30 to 35 minutes or until puffed and lightly brown.

7 Pierce each puff on its side with a fork to allow steam to escape. Cool completely.

8 To assemble cream puffs, split each with a sharp knife and dollop pudding mixture on bottom half.

9 Gently top with the other half and sprinkle with powdered sugar.

Mocha Filling

1 Combine pudding mix and milk in a heavy saucepan over medium heat and stir constantly.

2 Cook until thickened and then add coffee and stir well. Cover and refrigerate.

Chocolate Chip Oatmeal Raisin Cookies

MAKES 4 DOZEN LARGE COOKIES

½ cup **old-fashioned oats**

18.25-ounce box **German chocolate cake mix**

2 **eggs**

½ cup **butter**, melted

6 ounces **semisweet chocolate chips**

½ cup **golden raisins**

1 Place oats in a food processor and grind for 30 seconds.

2 Combine oats, cake mix, eggs and melted butter in a large mixing bowl and beat just until well blended.

3 Stir in chocolate chips and raisins and mix well. Batter will be thick.

4 Drop by rounded spoonfuls onto a cookie sheet, placing each cookie about 2 inches apart.

5 Bake at 350°F for 10 to 12 minutes.

6 Remove to a wire rack and cool.

7 Store in an airtight container.

Chocolate Almond Biscotti

MAKES 18 SERVINGS

1 cup **almonds**, sliced and toasted

1 cup **semisweet chocolate chips**

2 cups self-rising **flour**

¼ cup **cocoa**

¼ teaspoon **baking soda**

¼ teaspoon **salt**

½ cup **sugar**

½ cup **brown sugar**

3 large **eggs**

¼ cup **margarine**, softened

½ teaspoon **vanilla extract**

½ teaspoon **almond extract**

1 Spread almonds on an ungreased baking sheet and place in a 325°F oven for 12 minutes or until just toasted, not dark.

2 In a small glass bowl, melt chocolate chips in the microwave for about 1 minute, stirring midway.

3 Cool to room temperature.

4 Combine the flour, cocoa, soda and salt in a medium bowl and stir.

5 Combine the sugars, eggs, margarine and flavorings in a food processor and mix.

6 Add melted chocolate and process; gradually add flour and cocoa mixture and process.

7 Stir in nuts by hand.

8 Flour your hands, shape the dough into two 9x3-inch loaves and place on a greased baking sheet.

9 Bake in a 350°F oven for 30 minutes or until a knife inserted comes out clean.

10 Cool completely, then cut diagonally into ½-inch slices with a serrated knife.

11 Place slices onto a greased baking sheet and bake on one side for 10 minutes, then turn to the other side and continue baking for 10 minutes.

13 Remove from the oven and cool.

14 Store in an airtight container.

John's Nutty Carrot Cake

MAKES 10 SERVINGS

3 cups all-purpose **flour**

2¾ cups **sugar**

1 teaspoon **salt**

1 teaspoon **baking soda**

2½ teaspoons **ground cinnamon**

½ cup unsalted **butter**, melted

2 large **eggs**

1 cup **vegetable oil**

1 teaspoon **vanilla extract**

2 cups **walnuts**, chopped

1 cup **coconut**, shredded

1½ cups **carrots**, grated

1 cup **crushed pineapple**, drained

Cream Cheese Icing

2 8-ounce packages **cream cheese**, softened

⅔ cup **butter**, softened

6 cups **powdered sugar**

2½ teaspoons **vanilla extract**

1 Sift flour, sugar, salt, baking soda and cinnamon together in a large bowl.

2 Add butter, eggs, oil and vanilla extract and beat well.

3 Stir in the walnuts, coconut, carrots and pineapple; divide batter between 2 greased 9-inch cake pans.

4 Bake for 35 minutes at 350°F or until edges pull slightly away from the pan.

5 Cool completely on wire racks.

6 To assemble the cake, frost the bottom layer completely and put it in the freezer for 10 minutes until set.

7 Add the second layer and finish by frosting the top and sides.

8 Garnish with extra walnuts, if desired, and chill for an hour before enjoying.

Cream Cheese Icing

1 Beat cream cheese and butter together; add the powdered sugar and the vanilla extract and beat for 5 minutes.

2 Chill for 30 minutes.

From John Reliford, co-owner of Victoria Gardens in Louisville.

Dixie Peanut Brittle

MAKES 12 SERVINGS

2 cups **sugar**

1 cup **light corn syrup**

½ cup **water**

½ teaspoon **salt**

3 cups raw **peanuts**, shelled with the skins on

2 tablespoons **butter**

2 teaspoons **baking soda**

1 Line a baking sheet with foil and coat it with butter.

2 Heat sugar, syrup, water and salt in a heavy saucepan to a rolling boil, stirring constantly.

3 Add peanuts, reduce heat to medium and continue to stir.

4 Cook to hard crack stage (293°F).

5 Turn off the heat, add the butter and baking soda. Beat rapidly until well mixed.

6 Pour onto the buttered baking sheet, spreading the mixture to ¼-inch thickness.

7 Allow candy to cool completely; break into pieces and store in an airtight container.

David Dominé's Bourbon Ball Torte

MAKES 8 SERVINGS

4 ounces **bittersweet chocolate**
½ cup boiling **water**
1 cup **butter**, softened
2 cups **sugar**
4 large **eggs**, separated
1 teaspoon **vanilla extract**
2½ cups sifted cake **flour**
1 teaspoon **baking soda**
½ teaspoon **cinnamon**
½ teaspoon **salt**
1 cup **buttermilk**
¾ cup Kentucky **bourbon**

1 Preheat the oven to 350°F.

2 Break the chocolate into pieces and mix it with the boiling water until completely dissolved. Let cool.

3 Cream the butter and sugar until fluffy and pale yellow. Continue beating and add the egg yolks, one at a time, until thoroughly combined. Add the chocolate mixture and vanilla and mix well.

4 Sift together the flour, baking soda, cinnamon and salt.

5 Combine the buttermilk and bourbon.

6 To the butter-chocolate mixture, add half of the flour mixture and half of the buttermilk/bourbon mixture, continuing to mix and scrape the sides of the bowl.

7 Add the remaining buttermilk/bourbon mixture and flour mixture and mix on medium-high speed until smooth. Be careful not to over-beat the batter.

8 In a separate bowl, whip the egg whites at high speed until stiff peaks form.

9 Slowly fold the egg whites into the batter and pour into 4 buttered and floured 9-inch round pans. Bake on the center rack for 20 minutes or until a toothpick inserted in the center of the cake comes out clean. Remove from the oven and cool. Once the cakes have cooled, invert pans and turn them out.

David Dominé, aka The Bluegrass Peasant, is the dining correspondent for Kentucky Monthly. This recipe is from Dominé's cookbook, Splash of Bourbon: Kentucky's Spirit.

Filling
2 cups **heavy cream**
½ cup **powdered sugar**
16 large **bourbon balls**

Ganache
½ cup **heavy cream**
2 cups **semisweet chocolate chips**

Filling

1 Whip the cream with powdered sugar to form very stiff peaks.

2 Chop 8 of the bourbon balls into small pieces and add to the whipped cream. Chill for at least 1 hour so the filling can support the weight of the layers.

Assembling the Torte

1 Use a very sharp, serrated knife to cut off the tops of the cakes to produce 4 even layers.

2 Brush away excess crumbs from the tops of the cakes and place one layer on a large, flat plate.

3 Top the first layer with one-third of the filling and spread to within ¼ inch of the edge. Add the next layer and repeat the process.

4 Refrigerate the cake for at least 2 hours.

5 For the last stage of assembly, transfer the cake to a wire rack over a baking sheet and pour the ganache over the cake to coat completely.

6 Cool again, and once the ganache surface has solidified somewhat, decorate the top edge with the remaining bourbon balls.

Ganache

1 Scald the cream and add to the chocolate chips, whisking until completely melted and smooth.

Caramel Chocolate Pretzel Cookies

MAKES 60 COOKIES

13-ounce bag **Rolo candies**
60 Rold Gold **Tiny Twist pretzels**
60 **pecan halves**, toasted

1 Place pretzels on a parchment or foil-lined baking sheet.

2 Place 1 piece of candy on top of each pretzel.

3 Bake at 325°F for about 4 minutes or until the chocolate becomes shiny.

4 Remove the pan from the oven and gently press one pecan half onto each pretzel.

5 Cool for 10 minutes, and then place in refrigerator to set.

6 Store in a tin or airtight container.

Chocolate Chip Cheesecake Bars

MAKES 10-12 SERVINGS

16 ounces **cream cheese**, at room temperature
⅓ cup **sugar**
1 tablespoon **vanilla extract**
2 16.5-ounce refrigerated rolls of **chocolate chip cookie dough**

Chocolate Ganache Icing
1 cup of **semisweet chocolate chips**
¼ cup **whipping cream**

1 Place the cream cheese, sugar and vanilla extract in a bowl and combine with an electric mixer until creamy and smooth.

2 Slice 1 roll of the cookie dough and pat into the bottom of a greased 9x13-inch baking dish.

3 Smooth the cream cheese mixture over the dough.

4 Slice the second roll of dough and place it over the cheese mixture, pushing it down partway into the cheese.

5 Bake at 350°F for 20 to 30 minutes, or until top is slightly golden brown.

5 Cool and spread chocolate ganache icing over the top.

Chocolate Ganache Icing

1 Melt semisweet chocolate chips in a double boiler over medium-high heat.

2 Whisk ¼ cup whipping cream into the melted chocolate.

3 Let the mixture cool and thicken. Spread over the cheesecake.

Iris Moore's Crunchy Cookies

MAKES 6-8 DOZEN

1 cup **butter**

1 cup **sugar**

1 cup **brown sugar**, firmly packed

1 **egg**

1 cup **vegetable oil**

1½ cups **old-fashioned oats**

1 teaspoon **vanilla extract**

½ teaspoon **salt**

3½ cups self-rising **flour**

1 cup Post **Grape-Nuts**

1 cup grated **coconut**

1 cup **pecans**, chopped

1 Cream the butter and sugars together in a food processor or mixer until light and fluffy.

2 Add the egg, oil, oats, vanilla extract and salt and mix well.

3 Add ⅓ of the flour and mix.

4 Continue adding more flour until all flour is used and mix well. You may have to transfer it into a larger bowl and mix by hand with a large wooden spoon.

5 Pour in the Grape-Nuts, coconut and pecans and mix by hand.

6 Pinch off the dough and roll into balls the size of a quarter.

7 Place dough balls on an ungreased baking sheet and press down with a fork or with your hand.

8 Bake at 350°F for 10 to 12 minutes or until lightly browned.

9 Cool and store in an airtight container. These keep extremely well for two weeks or more.

Flan

MAKES 4 SERVINGS

12-ounce can **evaporated milk**
1 cup **sugar**
1 pinch of **salt**
2 teaspoons **vanilla**
4 **eggs**

1 Preheat oven to 350°F.

2 Caramelize four custard cup molds (see below).

3 Mix together the milk, sugar, salt and vanilla in a blender and blend.

4 Add the eggs to the blender one at a time and pulse rapidly.

5 Pour the mixture into caramelized custard cups and place the cups in a large pan.

6 Pour enough hot water into the large pan to come halfway up the sides of the cups.

7 Bake for one hour.

8 Remove the cups from the hot water and allow them to cool on a wire rack for approximately 30 minutes.

9 Once they have cooled, refrigerate until chilled.

10 When ready to serve, turn the flan over onto individual serving plates that are deep enough to hold the caramel syrup.

Caramelizing the Molds

1 Use 1 cup of sugar for 4 individual custard cups.

2 Place the sugar in a heavy, medium-size saucepan and place it over medium heat.

3 Hold the saucepan by the handle, turn and tip it gently until the sugar melts and becomes amber in color (looks like caramel).

4 Pour the caramel into the mold, and tip the mold back and forth to spread it evenly over the sides and bottom. The caramel does not have to cover the sides completely.

5 Set cups aside.

DERBY PARTY

Drink

Silky Sunshine
Cocktail (p. 142)

Desserts

Bourbon
Cheesecake
Brownies (p. 48)

or

Mint Julep
Cheesecake (p. 50)

or

Marsha Burton's
Woodford
Pudding (p. 63)

Appetizers

Derby Afternoon
Cheese Straws (p. 13)

and

Country Ham and Asparagus
Tartlets (p. 10)

or

Cheese and Bacon Stuffed
New Potatoes (p. 8)

Main Courses

Winning Ticket Breakfast
Casserole (p. 30) *and*

Sausage Cheese Grits (p. 31)

or

Shrimp Cakes with
Fresh Tarter Sauce (p. 36) *and*

Bluegrass Asparagus Salad (p. 22)

or

Country Ham Salad (p. 37) *and*

Steeplechase Pasta Salad (p. 28)

SUMMERTIME COOKOUT

Salads

Heirloom Tomatoes
with Green Goddess
Dressing (p. 74)

or

Mixed Greens with
Goat Cheese and
Blackberry Vinaigrette
(p. 72)

or

Honey Potato Salad
(p. 79)

Desserts

Chocolate Berry
Tart (p. 124)

or

Summertime Banana
Pudding (p. 136)

or

Summertime
Peach Pie (p. 138)

Main Courses

Best-Ever Baby Back Ribs (p. 98) *with*

Bourbon Chipotle Barbecue
Sauce (p. 101) *and*

Grilled Summer Squash and
Sweet Onions (p. 112)

or

Baked Barbecue Chicken (p. 102) *with*

Tex-Mex Corn on the Cob (p. 111) *and*

Red and Green Coleslaw (p. 116)

or

Grilled Bourbon Salmon (p. 92) *with*

Squash and Tomato
Casserole (p. 122) *and*

Asparagus with Lemon Zest (p. 128)

THANKSGIVING DINNER

Appetizers

Spicy Pecans (p. 146)

and

Austin's Inn Place
Spinach Parmesan
Clusters (p. 150)

Salads

Roasted Root Vegetables with
Bourbon Molasses Vinaigrette (p. 164)

or

Cranberry Salad with
Grapes and Apples (p. 167)

Desserts

Apple Bourbon
Upside-Down Cake
(p. 210)

or

The J.P. Rehm House
Chocolate
Chess Pie (p. 206)

or

Carrot Bars with
Cream Cheese
Frosting (p. 208)

Main Courses

Roast Turkey with Wild Rice and
Pecan Stuffing (p. 176)

served with

Bourbon-Braised Brussels Sprouts
with Bacon (p. 181) *and*

Sweet Potatoes in Orange Rinds (p. 194)

or

Broccoli and Cheese Casserole (p. 197) *and*

Stuffed Acorn Squash (p. 191)

or

Creamed Spinach (p. 196) *and*

Red Potato Casserole (p. 198)

HOLIDAY PARTY

Appetizers

Gruyere-Chive Mini
Popovers (p. 220)

or

Crostini with Steak
and Horseradish
(p. 224)

or

Hot Onion Soufflé
Appetizer (p. 226)

Desserts

David Domine's
Bourbon Ball
Torte (p. 260-261)

or

Cream Puffs with
Mocha Filling (p. 250)

Main Courses

Whole Beef Tenderloin (p. 244) *with*

Red Skin Garlic Mashed
Potatoes (p. 193) *and*

Green Beans with Caramelized Onions
and Bacon (p. 123)

or

Apricot Glazed Pork Chops with
Apricot-Apple Stuffing (p. 242) *and*

Delicious Carrots with White Grapes (p. 248)

or

Shrimp and White Asparagus
Casserole (p. 236-237) *and*

Walnut and Rosemary
Bread Loaves (p. 228-229)

With Gratitude

Putting together a cookbook is no small feat, and without the assistance of many individuals, this project of compiling a selection of recipes that have appeared in *Kentucky Monthly* magazine over the past three years would not have come together as seamlessly as it did.

We'd like to extend our appreciation to Michelle Stone and Paula Cunningham of McClanahan Publishing House, who provided many of the recipes for the magazine and thus this book. And a big thank-you to the chefs at Sullivan University, including Reagan D. Hamilton, C.C., for preparing many of the dishes for *Kentucky Monthly*; Glenn and Al Sullivan for kindly allowing the use of the university's facilities; Wales Hunter for his impeccable photography of these delectable delights; Art Director Kelli Schreiber for her always-imaginative and innovative design; Kendall Shelton for doing everything from making arrangements with the printer of the cookbook to the nitty-gritty of importing and formatting the text of the recipes; Rebecca Redding, for her design and layout assistance; and David Dominé, aka The Bluegrass Peasant, the dining correspondent for *Kentucky Monthly* and author of several cookbooks. Thanks also to those who copy-edited the book with eagle-eyed scrutiny: Kim Butterweck, Madelynn Coldiron, Patricia Ranft, Ted Sloan and Kay Vest.

We also are most grateful to those chefs and bed & breakfast proprietors who provided a number of sumptuous recipes: Rosalie Swann of Swann's Nest at Cygnet Farm in Lexington; Tina Emrick, co-owner of Sage Garden Café in Frankfort; Kathy Mayfield, who contributed the culinary sections for the book *Sterling Bits: Bluegrass Equestrian Experience*; Kathy Cary, chef and owner of Lilly's, A Kentucky Bistro, in Lousiville; Marsha Burton, owner of Louisville's 1853 Inn at Woodhaven; Austin's Inn Place in Louisville; Capt. Richard Bristol of Ft. Lauderdale, Fla.; Cynthia Lewis Jones of Lexington; Bob and Norma Laufer of Louisville's Carson House; Mike and Candace Milligan of The J.P. Rehm House in Louisville; and John Reliford of Louisville's Victoria Gardens.

Many thanks are to be extended to *Kentucky Monthly*'s loyal readers, a number of whom shared the secrets of their favorite dishes by entering the magazine's recipe contest or contributing to our Readers' Issue: Joan Sewell of Evansville, Ind.; Jean Merrell of Madisonville; Candy Charters of Frankfort; Beth and Steve Fischer of Frankfort; Charles Winter of Frankfort; Linda and Mike Hubbard of Lexington; Amandalin Ryan of Danville; Adam Johnson of Danville; Denise Scaringi of Lakeside Park; Connie Hervey of Alexandria; Connie Schuermeyer of Lexington; Jason Deatherage of Carrollton; Emily Braun of Cincinnati; and Sherree Loewenberg of Louisville.

And finally, a big thank-you to Stephen M. Vest, editor and publisher of *Kentucky Monthly*, without whom this book would not have been possible.